Staying Together

Books by William Glasser

Staying Together

THE CONTROL THEORY GUIDE
TO A LASTING MARRIAGE

WILLIAM GLASSER, M.D.

HarperPerennial

A Division of HarperCollins*Publishers*

First HarperPerennial edition published 1996.

Designed by Alma Hochhauser Orenstein

The Library of Congress has catalogued the hardcover edition as follows:

Glasser, William, 1925–
    Staying together : the control theory guide to a lasting marriage /
by William Glasser.
        p.   cm.
    ISBN 0-06-017247-9
    1. Marriage. 2. Control theory. 3. Man-woman relationships.
HQ734.G546   1995
158'.24—dc20   95-5745

ISBN 0-06-092699-6 (pbk.)

96 97 98 99 00 ❖/RRD 10 9 8 7 6 5 4 3 2 1

To Janet and Merle Fromson
and Joan and Frank Miller.

We were all members of
the marriage class of 1946.

Contents

Acknowledgments

When my wife, Naomi, passed away two years ago, I was left without an editor and, like almost all writers, I need an editor. If you believe this book reads clearly, it is because it is well edited, and the person I have to thank for this is Cynthia Merman. She was recommended by my publisher and, although I have never met her, I feel I know her well.

1

How It Began

Late in 1992, Naomi, my wife of forty-six years, died of cancer after a brief illness. We had a good relationship and were very close for the six months that she was ill. Before she died, we talked honestly about the future and how I would conduct my life with regard to our children, grandchildren, assets, and work, and I have not deviated from what I promised her. We also discussed my personal life and, knowing me so well, she told me that I would need a new relationship and she hoped I would find the right one. I didn't anticipate that the loneliness would be acute, but she was right. After all those years of marriage, I am not a good bachelor.

There are a lot of advantages to looking for love at an age when many of love's usual problems—money, children, not enough free time—no longer exist. Still, finding someone was not easy. I met fine women, but the right one eluded me. I am not naive where women are concerned and, as a psychiatrist, I know a little more than most about love and sex. I had a good idea of what I wanted, and I did not want to settle for less. I expected that there would be mistakes, and there were. From these mistakes, I learned a lot and began to toy with the idea of writing this book.

Then I got lucky. Carleen Floyd, from Cincinnati, was an instructor in my organization. I had known and admired her professionally for almost ten years. Now I learned that she was getting divorced, so I wrote her a letter.

I told her that I found her interesting and attractive and I sensed that the feeling was mutual. I suggested that I could visit her in Cincinnati and she could visit me in Los Angeles to see if we grew to love each other. I ended by saying that life is too short not to pursue excitement, adding that I believed Carleen and I could be exciting.

Carleen responded immediately—and positively. Two months later we got together for the first time in Cincinnati. We were powerfully attracted to each other and had what we agreed was close to a perfect weekend. We got together again Thanksgiving weekend at my home in Los Angeles and again in Cincinnati two weeks later, and things were still perfect. Two days before the New Year, even though we had made no plans to see each other over the holidays, I called and asked her to come to California. She came the afternoon of New Year's Eve.

When Carleen got back on the plane twenty-four hours later, it was no longer attraction—we were deeply in love and, equally important, we were becoming good friends. Inspired by that love and friendship, which continues stronger than ever, and in the hopes that what we have learned both before and after we met can be useful to others, I began this book.

2

Introducing Control Theory

Almost all of us fall in love, usually several times in our lives. Many fewer of us succeed in staying in love for any length of time. It is the same with sex. We find an exciting partner, but we cannot maintain the excitement. A good marriage (or long-term relationship) is the most difficult of all affiliations to maintain. Less than half of us are able to stay married for life. And of the half that do, few achieve the storybook "they lived happily ever after" ending.

Too many of us settle for much less. We stay together dissatisfied, long after both love and sex have all but disappeared. We do so for many reasons—children, money, religion—but it is the underlying pain, shame, and fear of breaking up and trying to start over that prevent us from divorcing or splitting up.

Since we all hope to keep love, sex, and marriage intact, we spend a lot of effort and even money trying to find out how to do this. We seek help ranging from Dear Abby to psychiatry, but much of this help is ineffective, usually because almost all of us are waiting for the helpers to tell us how to straighten out our partners. Few of the "experts" teach us that no matter what shape our relationship is in, only we can change. Also, most of us fail to see the obvious, which is that where sex, love, and marriage are concerned, the helpers for the most part are no more successful than the seekers.

The reason we are not taught that we must change is that almost all of us, including those who counsel the unhappily married, follow stimulus-response psychology, whose premise is that our unhappiness is caused by events or situations that are outside of ourselves. Simply stated, stimulus-response psychology leads us to believe that when we fail to find a successful relationship, it is someone else, not us, who is at fault.

Therefore, as we seek help from friends or professionals, we gain support for what we already believe: We are involved with the wrong mate and he or she must change for us to be happy. But we remain the same, our mate doesn't change, and our unhappiness continues. What we have to understand is that the only life we can control is our own and, in almost all instances, we can choose to change. Depending on what changes we make in our lives, there is a strong possibility that our mate also may choose to change. And if he or she changes in the right

direction, our marriages can become much better. Therefore, we can change only our own lives; we cannot
change what others do. It is to this vital truth that this
book is addressed. Lacking this knowledge, we enter
blindly into sex, love, and marriage, and many of us
crash.

To make the changes that we must make if we are to
improve our relationships, we must learn a lot more
about ourselves, and it is to this task that this book is
addressed. We will also learn a lot more about our mates
and our relationships. To do this, I introduce a new psychology, *control theory,* that you can put immediately to
work in your life. As you learn control theory and that
we are all control systems, you will be able to stop using
the destructive stimulus-response psychology that is the
cause of so much of the failure and unhappiness we
encounter in our relationships.

I have been studying and teaching control theory for
more than fifteen years. At first I taught it to counselors
and managers. It soon became apparent that the people
being counseled and managed needed to learn control
theory too. What is intriguing is that many counselors
and managers who learned this theory to use at work
told me that they found it very useful in every aspect of
their lives, especially in personal relationships such as
marriage. Although this theory does not tell you what to
do, it clarifies that you, as a control system, are choosing
all you do and, using this knowledge and other basics of
this theory, you learn to make better choices.

For example, many times in our marriages we feel
angry or depressed and, not knowing control theory, we

don't even consider the possibility that we are choosing to feel upset. We think it is happening to us because of what someone else is doing or failing to do. When we learn control theory, we discover that we do not have to continue to make these choices and, because of them, behave in ways that may destroy our marriages. Better choices are almost always available.

As we begin to act successfully on this new knowledge, we gain a sense of control over our lives, which feels very good. It is this sense of control—*over ourselves, not over others*—that gives control theory its name. Of course, we don't have to know control theory to struggle for control; we do that all the time both in and out of marriage. But until we learn control theory, we struggle to control others, not ourselves, and so we fail. Gradually, as we put control theory to work on ourselves, it becomes increasingly clear that applying the control theory axiom—*the only person we can control is ourself*—is vital if we are to have a chance for a more satisfying life.

Although I have written extensively on this theory, I realize that to apply this theory, especially to the problems of sex, love, and lasting relationships, I need to write in more depth about its most important concepts: the basic needs, total behavior, creativity, and, most of all, what I call our quality world. In this book, I apply these concepts to sexual relationships. But, as you learn them, you will find that they can be useful in every part of your life.

3

The Basic Needs and How They Relate to Our Personality

All living creatures struggle to stay alive at least long enough to reproduce so that their species continues to exist. Lower creatures are instructed by their genes to do this. For example, when salmon reach maturity, they struggle to return to the place where they were born. There, the females lay eggs, the males fertilize them, and then, exhausted by this effort and old age, both die. Few of us are unaware of this natural cycle and we know that salmon cannot choose to sit this struggle out. There is no escape from the suicidal reproductive behavior programmed into their genes.

As human beings, we have many more choices where reproduction is concerned. But for most of us, the urge to engage in sexual activity when we become sexually mature is as strong as that which drives the salmon to spawn. However this sexual program got written into our genes, it assures that from this activity enough human babies will see the light of day so there is little chance we will become an endangered species.

Even more obvious is the genetic program that urges us to eat and sleep. Babies don't have to be taught to pay attention to hunger and fatigue; the need to do so is programmed indelibly into their genes. The difference between humans and lower creatures is that lower creatures have more complex need-satisfying behaviors programmed into their genes. Salmon do not have to be taught to return to where they were born, the females to dig a hole for their eggs in the river bottom, the males to deposit their sperm on the eggs. These specific behaviors are mandated by their genes.

Humans have almost none of these programmed behaviors. Where reproduction is concerned, we, like a salmon, are given the urge to engage in sex, but, unlike a salmon, we have to learn how to do it. We also have to learn to take care of babies. If we had not learned to do this, our species would never have come into existence. We may have a "maternal instinct," but we still have to acquire caretaking skills.

But where behavior is concerned, we are not born with a blank genetic slate. As I explain in this chapter, what is programmed into our genes may be much less specific than what is written into the genes of fish or fowl, but what there is must be obeyed. From the standpoint of this book, the most important instructions written into our genes are five basic needs that we must attempt to satisfy all of our lives. To explain these needs, I must first explain our feelings.

If we agree that we all have a need to struggle to survive—for example, we attempt to find something to eat when we are hungry—what makes us continue to engage in the struggle is that it feels good to eat and feels bad not to eat. This simple concept is very important. Suppose we were born without the capacity to feel. From the standpoint of feelings, our lives are always the same, never good, never bad. How can we know we are hungry? How can we know that we have to eat? And if somehow we figured out that we needed to eat, how would we know how much to eat?

It is the hope of feeling good or better, immediately or later, that drives all of our behavior. In fact, as I explain later when I talk about total behavior, all behavior has a feeling component. For example, I look forward to eating because experience tells me that I will feel good as I satisfy my appetite. If the food I have available is tasteless, I may wait until I am very hungry and then eat only enough to relieve the hunger pangs. But it is still the hope of getting rid of the pain that drives my behavior.

So in humans, as in most higher animals, it is the capacity to know what feels good and what feels bad that drives all behavior. We may learn that eating meat feels very good and therefore we want to eat meat, but we do not have to learn that eating when we are hungry feels good. We experience and learn from that good feeling when we are fed as an infant, long before we are aware of what feelings actually are. Human babies also are aware that it feels good to rub their genitals long before they have any idea of sexual behavior.

We also have the capacity to learn and remember, and what we remember the longest is what we have experienced that feels best or worst. Based on these memories, our lives are dedicated to feeling good as often as we can and avoiding as much pain as possible in the process. What makes a need basic is that all direct attempts to satisfy this need are strongly associated with pleasure or pain. We know that it will feel very good to eat a tasty meal when we are hungry or to engage in satisfying sex almost any time. Where satisfying our basic needs is concerned, we can always count on feeling very good if we succeed.

For example, suppose a loving, satisfying partner suggests that we stop cleaning the house and make love. It is certainly desirable to live in a clean house, but who would say that to continue cleaning the house is the thing to do and later, if there is enough time, make love? There may be pressing reasons to postpone making love, although I can't think of any offhand, but I don't think anyone would say it will feel better to keep cleaning.

So it is how we feel as we behave that gives us vital information about the state of satisfaction of our needs. The only need that I have dealt with so far is our need to survive as individuals and as a species, but if we are economically secure and have an available sexually satisfying partner, we would likely feel good a lot of the time. There are four other basic needs that, unsatisfied, alter the above scenario. But before I explain them, I need to explain some elementary genetics so that it is clear what I am talking about when I mention our genetic structure.

Human Eggs, Sperm, and the Genes That They Contain

When the sperm and the egg combine in the woman's fallopian tube to make the single cell that will in the course of 280 days, if all is normal, divide and subdivide the billions of times that it takes to make a baby, each contributes about 50,000 genes to the first cell that starts the process. It is these 100,000 genes that are the instructions for the anatomy and physiology of that first cell and all subsequent cells. As all the cells that follow the first cell come into being, a copy of these 100,000 initial genes is replicated in every cell. If all goes normally, those genes intruct each cell to become what it needs to become: hair cells become hair, brain cells become brain, etc.

The cells are instructed by the appropriate gene or genes in both their structure and their function, and a normal baby is born with normal anatomy and physiology. Geneticists, however, have determined that it takes only about 10,000 genes to perform this function, which leaves 90,000 genes unaccounted for. What I propose in my explanation of control theory is that some of these "excess" genes, unconcerned with structure and physiologic function, tell us in general ways how we must attempt to live our lives.

Specifically, written into our genes are five basic

instructions that I call basic needs. From birth to death, we are instructed by these genes to try to (1) survive as individuals and to reproduce so we survive as a species, and to find (2) love and belonging, (3) power, (4) freedom, and (5) fun. For all practical purposes, our genes do not provide us with any specific behaviors to do this. Soon after birth we start learning how to behave, and we continue learning better ways the rest of our lives. As explained, to do this we are given the ability to feel both pleasure and pain, specifically to be able to tell quickly one from the other. Therefore, anything we do that feels good feels that way because it is satisfying to one or more of these five basic needs. Conversely, anything we do, or fail to do, that feels bad is unsatisfying or insufficiently satisfying to one or more of these same five needs.

Our total biologic incentive is to feel as good as we can as soon and as often as we can. Almost all of us, however, learn that it sometimes feels better or hurts less in the long run to suffer for a while now in exchange for feeling better later. Our genes, however, are not completely selfish, and we are far from totally hedonistic. Many of us deprive ourselves or do things that are painful in order to help others. We do these things because we think they are right or moral and because in the end we believe or hope that we will feel better.

The Basic Needs and Morality

Given that we are driven by five basic needs that force us to attempt to satisfy them, it is necessary to understand that there is nothing moral or immoral about this biologic process. The process is neutral. However, we may attempt to satisfy our need to survive at the expense of other people. For example, in the classic crowded lifeboat problem where some survivors must be thrown overboard or all will drown, the strong usually dominate the situation and decide who will be sacrificed. All kinds of moral arguments for and against what the strong did can be made later but, in most cases, their need to survive dominated the same need of the weak, arguably not the most moral way to solve the problem.

As I discuss the needs, I will point out that morality is a human choice, not a genetic instruction, and often, as in the lifeboat example, it pits one need, survival (and to some extent power), against another, love and belonging. How a moral decision is arrived at is rarely predictable. All that is predictable when needs are in conflict is that there will be moral problems and that there is no absolute morality. For example, almost everyone believes in the commandment "Thou should not kill," but there are countless exceptions, such as self-defense, to that decree.

If everyone could satisfy his or her needs all the time there would be no moral problems. But, in fact, few of us can satisfy all our needs even most of the time, so we are continually forced to choose between satisfying one need at the expense of another. Control theory cannot offer morality, but it can offer knowledge. If we know about the needs and also know that, like all natural processes, they will vary in strength from one person to another, we can use this knowledge to help us make moral decisions. Simply stated, we cannot change our needs, but we can change the ways we try to satisfy them. (I discuss this subject in detail in chapter 6 when I explain the quality world.)

The Need to Survive, the Most Physiologic of Our Basic Needs

This universal need, shared by all living things, manifests itself in many ways. Some of the most obvious are physiological—eating, sleeping, keeping warm, and hormone-driven sex for species survival—which I have already discussed. But for humans there are less obvious and more psychological ways that have a lot to do with how many of us decide to live. For example, a person with a strong need to survive tends to be very conservative, take few risks, save rather than spend, be concerned with security, stick with his or her own kind, value the status quo, and distrust new things, new ideas, and new people. Survival-dominated people tend doggedly to follow common sense, even if it does not seem to work very well in some instances.

This is not to say that there is anything wrong with being this way: It is safe and secure. But survival-dominated people often run into trouble when they are confronted with a parent, mate, or profligate child who is much less dominated by survival genes. The problem is that we can't choose our relatives; we are stuck with them. And even though they are closer to us genetically than those we choose, such as our mates or friends, due to normal genetic variance their genetic structure can be far different from ours.

As I explain later, if we can learn how our genes may control our personality, we may be able to use this information to choose partners who are more compatible with our personality than are our relatives. For example, it would be useful to be able to recognize that someone we are attracted to has a far greater or lesser need to survive than we have. Although I cover these common situations in some detail shortly, it is obvious that this would not be a wise marriage. It is genetically predisposed to conflict and, as a psychiatrist, I have seen my share of troubled marriages where these (and other) need-genes were incompatible.

The sad part is that savers and spenders are often attracted to each other because each hopes that love will overcome the other's shortcomings and his or her way of living will prevail. This is asking a lot of love, more than it can usually deliver. These marriages, even if they stay together—and they usually do because the survival-dominated partner abhors divorce—are rarely happy.

Therefore, it is not only knowledge of the needs themselves but also their strength that is a concern. It is the strength of the needs that forms our personality, a topic I discuss in detail in chapter 5.

Love and Belonging: The First Psychological Need

As I explained when I discussed survival, even this basically physiological need has many psychological implications when it comes to getting along with others. But it is the psychological ramifications of the remaining needs—love, power, freedom, and fun—that present us with the most problems as we attempt to maintain relationships. Just because a need must be satisfied psychologically, as love and belonging certainly must, this does not make the psychological instructions less urgent than survival. For example, humans are essentially the only creatures that knowingly commit suicide, and it is obvious that no creature dominated by survival—as most animals are—could commit suicide.

From studying suicide, especially the notes that people leave behind, it appears that people who kill themselves are having great difficulty satisfying one or more of their psychological needs for love, power, and freedom. But most of the evidence points to their inability to find sufficient love. In their notes they say that they do not have and do not expect to have enough love to make their lives worth living. The pain of living with insufficient love is more than they can bear, and suicide is the way they get rid of this pain.

How much we need love is graphically illustrated by the fact that a novel purely about love and its associated problems, *The Bridges of Madison County,* has been on the hardback bestseller list (more than two million copies sold) for several years. Loneliness is certainly among the most painful of all human experiences, and a lot of readers, especially women, identify with the book's lonely heroine and are thrilled by the strength of her brief but intense sexual experience. The popularity of this book also indicates that a lot of people, again mostly women, want not more sex but more loving sex.

The success of *Bridges* illustrates clearly the point of

this book, which is that even though we all want love and a sense of belonging, many of us have difficulty figuring out how to get what our genes tell us we need. It would seem that if we all want it so much, it would be easy to find. But it isn't. To get sufficient love we have to depend on another person, yet we have no control over other people. Your telling me you love me does not at all ensure that I will feel the same about you. Sufficient love also is difficult to find because there are wide differences in how much each of us considers sufficient.

Women, probably based on their role as mothers, seem to need more love than men and, statistically, tend to marry men who do not need as much love as they do. When a woman marries a man who is satisfied with considerably less love and attention than she wants, both partners will be frustrated: she, because he doesn't give enough; and he, because his lesser need makes it difficult for him to understand why she both gives and wants so much. Thus, as in survival, people vary considerably in the amount of love programmed into their genes.

A man with a strong survival need will want a lot of sex and, in the beginning, will act loving to get it. His partner, also driven by the need for survival, will want sex too. Both are fooled by this early, intense sexuality. But if he has a moderate need for love and she a high need for it, she will soon detect that something is missing and may withdraw. He, in his frustration, may withdraw in return, and the marriage suffers. Since most people do not understand this, they base their marriages on hope instead of on trying to find out if they are compatible in the amount of love each needs.

There is another problem. One partner, usually the woman, recognizes that the other partner needs less love and is even attracted by this. Driven by her strong need for love, she believes that she will be able to love him so much that her love will bring out a latent need that she is sure is there. But in most cases it is not latent, it is not there at all, and these marriages are usually miserable.

There are variations. Many women and men are very loving toward children yet seem unable to love an adult with that same intensity. This may be because children, especially small children, need so much attention and care, which is very satisfying to give, and parents do not expect to get very much in return from a small child. Just seeing the child happy is usually enough.

As children grow older, we begin to expect more from them, and with adults—mates or children—we almost always expect more in return for what we give. When we don't get what we expect, we are less able or willing to create a loving adult relationship, and our relationships with adult, nonloving children, whom we cannot divorce, are often as painful and disappointing as a nonloving marriage.

Sex also presents problems. Any behavior that is repeated with the same person over and over tends to become boring because we know what to expect. There are two ways to solve this problem: Look for a new partner or bring some creativity into the old relationship. In my observation, most people look for or fantasize about a new partner. Fantasizing is by far the safest way, as exemplified by the warm reception even "sophisticated" people gave to *The Bridges of Madison County*. The less sophisticated have made the authors and publishers of Harlequin Books rich from these same fantasies.

But many people, especially those people with a strong need for both survival and love, have too many hormones and too much desire for real human contact to be satisfied by fantasies. Driven by the need for sexual love, and presented with what seems to be a good opportunity, they find a partner outside the marriage, as did Francesca in *Bridges*. But this book also illustrates another truth: Even with short- or long-term exceptions, we are generally a survival-driven, monogamous society. Affairs are dangerous to our security and, in the end, Francesca settled for her fantasies. It is more common to go from one monogamous relationship to another than to have several sexual partners at the same time.

Unfortunately, the heavy media emphasis on "great sex" raises expectations that few people in long-term monogamous relationships can realize. Some people cope by engaging in long-term affairs that seem similar to monogamy but are much more sexually satisfying for several reasons. First they tend to select extramarital partners more carefully than spouses and tend to choose ones with similar needs. And because of the need for secrecy, they tend to treat them better. Second, for long-term sex with the same partner to be satisfying, the partners have to keep sex on their mind, and people who engage in secret affairs keep sex very much on their mind, which gives an affair this peculiar sexual advantage.

Keeping a long-term secret affair usually demands creativity on the part of both partners, and shared creativity is highly satisfying. And since sex with a desirable, genetically compatible partner is inherently very satisfying, the creative aspects of an affair add layer after layer of icing to the cake. The necessary distractions of marriage often get in the way of sex. These distractions are eliminated in an affair, which further adds to its appeal, so that many who engage in this activity believe the risk is worth it.

The faithful partners, whether the affair is known to them or not, may feel that they are struggling in an unfair fight. Given the routines of marriage that are absent in an affair, they are right. This is often seen when they get divorced and what was an affair becomes a marriage with all its attendant realities. A husband who comes to pick up the children often looks wistfully at his ex-wife who, especially if she has found a lover, looks much better than she did when he was married to her.

You may be thinking that I have made affairs sound too attractive. What I have actually made attractive is a loving, creative sexual relationship, about the most attractive thing there is in the world. However, I am not suggesting that this is available only outside of marriage. There may not be enough happy marriages, but there are many. What makes them happy is that the partners work to create what I have just described. It is not programmed into our genes like spawning; we have to learn how to do it. Most of us don't learn how to love sufficiently, and this is why marriages fail and affairs occur. Control theory supplies some of what we need to know.

Finally, and this is the heart of control theory, no human being wants to be controlled by another human being. When I discuss the need for power, I point out that almost all people attempt to satisfy it by trying to control others. This is never a satisfactory way to relate to anyone—friends seem to understand this and good friends tend to be tolerant and noncontrolling—and it is especially disastrous where love and sex are concerned. Loving sex is giving, and control is taking. So running a power trip on another person hurts love and kills most opportunities for good sex. Where both partners are doing it, satisfying sex becomes almost impossible.

Another attraction of an affair is that it is very difficult to control the partner in a secret relationship. The partner can quit anytime he or she wants. Most people do not even choose to risk an affair with someone who is trying to control them, and affairs where one or the other is trying to control quickly run their course. Affairs are almost always based on the search for more love.

If a married woman or man suspects or becomes aware that a partner is involved in an affair, control theory strongly suggests that the best strategy is to make no effort to control the wandering spouse. If you are in this situation, keep in mind that you are still married. The infidelity may cause you to choose a lot of misery, but your partner has not left. Your job is to figure out how you can become more attractive, to bring into your relationship what is being sought with someone else.

Unfortunately, applying common-sense stimulus-response psychology to this situation leads the offended partner to become more demanding and controlling and thus even less attractive. Control theory often suggests that we act exactly the opposite to what common sense urges us to do, that we use the lessons of control theory to create a new common sense.

Power: The Second Psychological Need

If we look at dogs, we can easily see that they are driven by the need to survive—few dogs miss a meal or a chance for a nap—as well as by a strong need for love and, when young, for fun. Unlike their close relatives, wolves, dogs seem to have had the need for freedom mostly bred out of their genes. Some roam a little, but given a loving home, they tend to stick around.

With their human masters, dogs seem almost devoid of the need for power. Most breeds can be easily trained to do what they are told, for example, to stay, more than almost any other higher animal. Dogs appeal to us because they willingly, even eagerly, subject themselves to our will, especially if we give them the love they strongly crave. We, on the other hand, are by far the creature most driven by the need for power. Just look at the front page of any newspaper—almost every article is about the search for power.

For example, the front page of today's *Los Angeles Times* has nine stories, and six are about power: A rebellion in Mexico is the headline piece; increasing fees to gun dealers to make guns less accessible is just below it. The others are the exploitation of Indian children in New Delhi; the merger of two large department stores; how lobbyists, not equity, run the city government; and how the White House is hesitant to admit government liability for using people in radiation experiments. In all these instances the need for power is the major driving force, and this need will continue to make more news than all other needs combined. I concede that survival and freedom are mixed into the stories—there is almost never any love or fun on the front page—but power is obviously dominant.

Most of us are not concerned with the kind of power that makes the front page. Even though almost all of us would like to have more money or prestige, our power need generally is satisfied if we are respected. To gain respect, the minimum is that someone we care about, usually our partner, listens to us. If we don't have that, almost all of us struggle to get it and, if this struggle persists, we stop loving our partner. We may be so frustrated that we end a marriage, or we may stay in this frustrating situation but get little out of it except some satisfaction from an active or passive struggle with our mate.

Our need for power makes it hard for us to accept a low-power position in any relationship, particularly a marriage. Although I cover this in much more detail in chapter 8, I believe the greatest obstacle to a happy marriage is the inability of one or both partners to satisfy their need for power in the partnership. It is rarely the lack of love that destroys relationships: It is more that love cannot take root in a relationship in which one or both of the partners believe they have too little or no power.

For a partnership to succeed, the partners must also be friends. In a romantic relationship, friendship is usually preceded by love and sex. But if friendship is not quickly and firmly established, love soon withers. More than anything else, friendship is based on equal power, and equal power is based on listening to each other, really paying attention. There is no other way.

My colleagues and I see this need for power every day in our practices. Virtually all of our clients say over and over how empowering it is to be able to talk to someone who actually listens to them and takes them seriously.

As in survival and love, the power genes in each of us follow a normal distribution. Some of us are much more driven by power than others, and anyone strongly driven by power may find marriage difficult to tolerate, especially if married to a high-power partner. High-power men tend to be sexually attractive to women, especially women with a fairly strong power drive themselves. Henry Kissinger said, "Power is the ultimate aphrodisiac," and he was in a position to know.

But a good marriage needs more than an aphrodisiac; it needs friendship. And it is rare for a powerful man to be good friends with a powerful wife; they are too much in competition. Therefore, when powerful women marry powerful men, the marriage may last but love and sex suffer. The marriage between Eleanor and Franklin Roosevelt comes to mind. They did not divorce but did turn to less powerful people for love.

When one mate has a high need for power, his or her marriage has the best chance for success if the other has much less of this need. In these marriages, there is less conflict and some low-power partners are even able to bask in their mate's success. There are numerous examples of older, usually rich and powerful people, who are successfully married to younger mates. My guess is that the younger person has less of a power drive and enjoys the power of the spouse. With this need pattern, they are not in conflict and may become good friends, and as a result they may enjoy a good sexual relationship.

This is in contrast to survival, where two people with high survival needs are a good combination. If they both have low survival needs, this too may work. But if one is a spender, the other a saver, this bodes poorly for the marriage. It is the same—or even more so—for love. Couples with an equal need for love have a good chance for a happy marriage. But when a high-love person and a low-love person marry, this leads quickly to frustration.

The best marriages may be between people who both have a weak to moderate need for power and, at least, an average need for love. They listen to each other without trying to control, and the chances for conflict are much less than if both have a high need for power. The problem is that these low-power people do not often serve as the role model for a good marriage: They are not the stuff that books and movies are written about. Scarlett and Rhett were great characters, but Ashley would have made Scarlett a better husband.

It is also more difficult to assess one's own or another's need for power than to figure out survival and love requirements. This is because when we struggle for power, we will often behave lovingly in order to seduce the partner into giving us what we want.

Nevertheless, when I discuss how our personality is formed in chapter 5, I attempt to explain how we can assess the strength of our needs as well as the strength of the needs of others. To do this accurately before getting married is of course best, but to do it after marriage still provides information vital to the success of any relationship.

Freedom: The Third Psychological Need

All living creatures, most without knowing they do this, struggle to be free to live as they think best. We, of course, are very aware of this struggle, and history is full of groups of people who succeeded in gaining their freedom. Since all of us are struggling for control, this struggle for freedom often takes the form of attempting to get out from under the control of others. To make what they do more palatable, many power-driven people who harm others claim that they are fighting for freedom. Therefore, most prominent in all human relationships is the continual struggle between freedom and power. Our genes themselves are the basis for much of this conflict.

By its very nature, any intimate relationship is frustrating to our need for freedom—if I give you love, then you must pay attention to what I want. When I was young, a wife was frequently referred to as a "ball and chain." The term "free love," less heard now in the age of HIV (human immunodeficiency virus), referred to the joy of loving partners who made no attempt to restrict each other's freedom, quite opposite from what goes on in most marriages. Therefore, it seems fairly obvious that people who have low freedom needs have a much better chance for a successful marriage than those with a high need for independence.

Most of the rage that erupts in marriage and may lead to battering is caused by one partner, almost always the man, feeling powerless outside the marriage. The only power he is able to gain is through dominating his wife and children. There is almost nothing that they can do in this instance; even complete submission will not give him the power he needs. And if the police are involved, he will feel even less powerful and more resentful. Anything less than total intervention will be unsuccessful.

But sometimes anger erupts when one partner, again usually the male, has less of a need for love and a much higher need for freedom than the other partner. To get the love and loving sex that he wants, he has to give up some freedom and this is very hard to do. His wife may nag him for more help with the children and more companionship. She may become less interested in sex, which is also frustrating for him. She is either unaware or unwilling to accept his high need for freedom, and though her constant nagging makes things worse, she may be unwilling to stop. As more and more he sees himself trapped and couples this frustration with drinking, violence is often the result. Freedom and love are not necessarily in conflict, but if the love is insufficient, they usually are.

It is not uncommon for divorced people to get back together when both parties can enjoy each other sexually without the constraints of marriage. Those who are fooled by this rekindling of sexual desire and remarry usually find that they have made a serious mistake. They quickly lose what made their newfound attraction possible. Their second marriage soon becomes identical to their first.

Other than a low need for freedom on the part of both partners, it is hard to figure out what level of freedom makes for a good marriage. If both partners have a high need for freedom, the marriage can work if they are able to recognize and accept that this is what they both need. I am not talking about sexual freedom—few people accept this—but rather about personal freedom.

Suppose a man who spends weekends skiing marries a woman who has no interest in outdoor sports but is an amateur photographer. If both have a high need for freedom, they might easily accept that each needs time to pursue his or her separate interests. If they not only allow but encourage the other to do what each wants, the time they spend together can be very satisfying and the marriage successful.

But usually it is people with dissimilar needs for freedom who marry. If they don't understand that this is the case—and most don't—those marriages suffer as the person with the low need for freedom cannot understand why the other is not satisfied to stay at home. These marriages may continue, but the freedom-driven person may have to drown his or her pain in drinking and television, a compromise that brings no happiness to either partner.

As I discuss in chapter 5, the needs do not necessarily exert their individual influence as strongly as I have been discussing. For example, a very high need for love that is satisfied might keep a strong need for power and/or freedom in check. But what I want to emphasize, in terms of all the needs, is that they do exert a strong influence and, when frustrated, force us into injurious behavior.

Fun: The Fourth Psychological Need

We are born with powerful needs but not with the behaviors to satisfy them. Unlike lower creatures—the salmon, for example—that can take care of themselves at birth, we are born with only a few primitive behaviors such as crying, coughing, and sneezing. We are also the creatures most involved in playing.

Young, lower animals such as dogs and cats also seem to expend a lot of energy playing and seemingly trying to have fun. But as they mature in good homes, they revert mostly to the survival activities of eating and sleeping; they may lose their sex drive due to spaying or neutering. Animals in the wild, with perhaps the exception of primates, whales, and dolphins, also play when young, but when they mature, they stick pretty much to survival activities that, including sex, don't look like much fun. Of course, I am putting my brain into an animal, which may be highly inaccurate.

As I was thinking about why we struggle so much for fun, I watched a National Geographic television special on sea turtles. As the turtles went through their life cycles, it seemed to me that if ever a creature lived a serious no-play, nonfun existence, this one did. It struck me that the reason for their serious life is that turtles are born knowing almost all they ever have to know.

This is a different situation from animals like dogs and cats, who have to learn a lot and much of whose play simulates what they are to use later. Once mature, they, or their genes, decide that they now know all they have to know and, unless it is to please a human they love, most of them don't play anymore.

What I have concluded is that play and fun provide the genetic reward for learning anything new that might immediately or at some later date be useful. For example, Hank Benjamin, a fourth-grade schoolteacher in Michigan who works extensively with my ideas, offers to teach his pupils to play chess, and almost all accept. Although chess, like all games, satisfies the need for power if we win often enough, most of his pupils do not pursue chess seriously. They do, however, learn from this effort to appreciate learning and that it takes effort to learn well. Benjamin also emphasizes writing and believes that what his students learn from chess helps them with this necessary life skill. This must be true, because I have never read better writing from pupils of this age than what he has sent me.

It is obvious that we do not have a chess, algebra, or literature gene, but we do have a set of learning genes that, when we learn anything that is need satisfying, cause us to feel good. And when we feel good, we believe it is because we are having fun. Sometimes it is play, sometimes not, but it is hard to play without learning, and huge sums of money are spent by very ordinary athletes on golf and tennis lessons. Their major motivation is to have fun: If they seek power, most will be disappointed. Evolution favored those who learned the most, so as we evolved we were given a set of fun-loving, learning genes.

People have asked me, How do I know I am having fun? My answer is that you find yourself laughing a lot. In my work in schools, I talk to hundreds of students and I always ask them, "What do good teachers do?" Invariably the answer is, "They make school fun" or "They make learning fun." Students also mention the other needs by explaining: "They talk with us and listen to us" (power). "They care about us" (love). "They give us a chance to do what we want to do" (freedom). The students don't mention survival: In this context the other needs predominate, and fun seems to be the most important of all.

It should be clear that sharing a strong need for fun is supportive to all human relationships and certainly is necessary for a successful marriage. It can add a great deal of strength to the love-cement that binds two people together. A fun-loving person who marries a sourpuss will regret this mistake the rest of his or her life. The sourpuss may not like it, but he or she won't suffer, and may even enjoy the spouse to some extent, but not to the extent of giving up his or her gloomy ways.

But, as mentioned, there is a serious side to fun: It is the reward for learning. What is necessary for a good relationship is that the partners share some common interest and learn together. For example, couples who both like to travel can plan, learn, and look forward for a year or more to a great trip during which they visit and study firsthand what they have learned. I know many people, mostly women, who travel by themselves because their husbands hate to travel or don't want to travel where their wives want to go. These husbands, not strongly driven by the need for fun, don't have much interest in learning new things about the world.

I say this because fun-loving people are interested in everything; the less-fun-loving have much more limited interests. The more the interests a couple shares, the better the chances that their marriage won't go stale and they won't start living separate intellectual lives. The key to friendship is sharing and expanding common interests and, at the risk of being repetitious, friendship is the key to a good marriage. If you are a fun-loving person, make sure that you hook up with a person who has a similar need for fun.

Fun has great staying power. Sex and love may wane over a long marriage, but fun remains fresh because, unlike sex, it can always go in a new direction. We all know people who have found an interest later in life that has transformed them. If they are fortunate enough to be able to share their interest and their enthusiasm with their partner, even if the partner only listens with interest, they have discovered one of the vital secrets of a long and happy marriage. Don't discount fun. It is the easiest of the needs to fulfill, since it is the only one that can be satisfied by oneself without much complaint from most partners.

Recreation: Our Specific Search for Fun

Partners who share a hobby or recreation have a good chance of maintaining a happy relationship. But this is not as easy as it sounds because recreational tastes vary widely. For example, mountain climbing is very satisfying to four needs: survival, belonging, power, and fun. Many people get a thrill in risking their lives (survival) roped together (belonging) on the side of a mountain. They feel powerful when they "conquer" the peak, and all the learning and preparation are fun. Since this is necessarily a cooperative effort, there is no individual freedom in it. But the whole group gets a satisfying sense of freedom. For the spouse who stays home, the main thrill may be in getting his or her partner back alive, which is hardly conducive to a good marriage.

Women generally are less driven by power than men and do not enjoy power-satisfying recreation, active or spectator, as much. Violent spectator sports, especially football, boxing, and hockey, are more male satisfying; basketball and tennis are more female satisfying. There are, of course, many exceptions to this generalization, but women who are aware that they have less of a need for power than the men they are attracted to should try early in the relationship to find a compatible recreation. If not, it is unlikely to surface later. Loneliness from being unable to find enjoyable things to do with their husbands is a common complaint of many wives who marry men with a much stronger power drive.

Men with moderate needs for power are more likely to enjoy intellectual recreations like travel, theater, art, and music. Almost the worst thing someone can do is nag a partner to do what he or she does not want to do. This is less likely to occur if the power needs are similar. So even though I argued that men with a high power need are better off with women with a low power need in terms of who calls the shots in the marriage, this is not true if the men don't recognize their wives' greater need for fun. Women do not usually divorce successful, power-driven mates, but the marriages are unhappy much of the time unless they find mutually enjoyable things to do together.

4

Sex, Sexual Love, and the Basic Needs

Sex is on the minds of most people, especially those who shouldn't be having it. Lurid sex is always news, and the more public figures are involved, the bigger the story. The quest for sex is the bread (violence is the butter) of Hollywood, and when sex is shown on the screen it must fall within the following unwritten law: Restrict it to the unmarried. This, however, is more showbiz than immorality. There is just no way to depict a long-term, sexually satisfying relationship so that anyone would be interested.

The obvious reason for this intense interest in sex is that huge numbers of people, married as well as single, are frustrated because they have not figured out how to maintain an exciting sexual relationship. They look for or fantasize about exciting sex in the mistaken belief that, if somehow they can find it, this time it will last. But it won't. Sex by itself, even initially exciting sex, has no staying power.

In their quest for excitement, many people turn to sex advice books. But most of the advice focuses on the wrong thing: Change the way you do it. It doesn't focus on what is really needed for long-term exciting sex: how to find a person we love who loves us. This requires a lot more knowledge about people than about sex. If you want to learn more about people and relationships, control theory can provide some answers.

If we can find someone we love who loves us, and if we are able to combine this love with sex, there is a good chance we will enjoy what many people believe is the ultimate intimate experience: sexual love. Finding this is a lot more difficult than just finding sex because it can be experienced only in *relationships where the lovers are very good friends*. And if our high divorce rate indicates anything, it is that many people cannot figure out how to become friends or stay friends with a long-term sexual partner.

Friendship is based on sharing common interests, being able to say what's on your mind without fear of rejection or criticism, planning and building a life together, and most of all looking forward to being with each other when there is nothing pressing to do. And a good friend supports the interests of a partner even when they are not shared. Someone you can talk with anytime about anything is the ultimate in marital friendship. There are too many married strangers.

My experience as a psychiatrist, with many people who were dissatisfied sexually, is that they are not good friends with the person they are trying to make love with. Some have never been good friends. They do not love their partner because they do not even like him or her. They admit that it is easier to make love with a stranger or a new acquaintance because, with someone new, if love is what they want, there is always the hope of finding it. There is none of the sex-destroying antipathy that tends to build in sexual relationships in which there is little or no friendship.

My experience in dealing with impotent men and frigid women supports this logic. The problem is usually not total—it is person specific. They either don't like their mate enough or are nervous or tentative because they do not believe that their mate likes them enough, fearing that if they fail to perform or reach orgasm, their mate will not continue to love them. When they change lovers or masturbate, the problem disappears. The mechanism is intact; it is caring or confidence with this partner that is lacking.

Sometimes impotence or frigidity occurs in a marriage where there seems to be genuine caring, which may be because one or both cannot relax, expecting too much of oneself. It is generally recognized that for good performance, the participants must be relaxed; if they try too hard, they fail. But the more they think, I care for this person so it should work, the harder they try and the more frustrated they become. Long-term sex works when the partners care for each other enough that performance is never demanded. They are continually able to send the message: We will not demand what one or the other finds difficult to do. There may still be failures, but, eventually, when impotent or frigid people feel loved and accepted no matter what happens, they expect less of themselves and things get better.

Therefore, it is dislike or fear of dislike that makes long-term satisfying sex difficult. If the couple who are having difficulty making love can gain or regain some friendship and love, the sex may return, as it often does when people who care for each other make up after an argument or a fight. Trying to fix the sex without paying attention to the lack of friendship is rarely successful.

Sex is often on our minds because it relates to all of our needs. For example, based on our need to survive, many of us engage in a lot of hormonal sex, especially when we are young. There is nothing wrong with hormonal sex. It can be physically very satisfying. But because it is so physical, it is usually short term. If one or both partners want love, the sex is unsatisfying and the relationship ends.

There is a lot of power sex. Movie stars, rock stars, and star athletes are much sought sexually and many tend to engage in a lot of short-term relationships. Most of the groupies who pursue these people in the hopes of sharing a little bit of their power may fantasize that love will follow, but it rarely does. Love requires friendship and respect, and those who use their power for sex rarely respect their partners.

Still, powerful people are very attractive sexually and, if they also care for their partner, the combination of power and love can be very satisfying for a long time.

Powerful people, who do not have any difficulty attracting sexual partners, often find it difficult to settle for one person when so many clamor for their attention. This is the chance that their partners take, but many recognize this and are willing to take the chance.

Driven by a strong need for freedom, many people who engage in a lot of sex refuse to restrict themselves to marriage. If they do enter into a relationship, they rarely give the lesser-freedom partner the commitment he or she wants. These are the couples who live together but break up without getting married. Marriages in which one or both partners have a high need for love and freedom are challenging, but they frequently last if the partners can work out a nonsexual way for the freedom-loving partner, or partners, to have what he or she wants.

Love and fun, because fun and friendship are so closely associated, seem to go together. People who have high needs for love and fun find that sex is an ideal way to satisfy them. Fun lends creativity and innovation to the activity, and loving couples who can incorporate a lot of fun into their lovemaking may be the most able to enjoy long-term, satisfying sex. Sex can also be satisfying for a while without much love, since being creative and intimate with another person is almost always a lot of fun.

But when fun without love drives these relationships, the sex is usually short term; one or both partners want more. If both partners have a strong need for love, love may grow quickly in what was initially a fun relationship. When fun is the instigator, there is much more of a chance for love to grow than when the sex is initiated by survival, power, or freedom.

Few if any highly pleasurable activities are able to satisfy all the needs as much as sex does. Gambling comes close in that gamblers are driven by power and also, to some extent, by freedom and fun. Gambling, however, is the antithesis of love and survival. Dedicated gamblers tend to have little interest in sex and no interest in long-term sex.

Alcoholics and other drug users tend to be normal in their needs but have trouble satisfying them. They discover that alcohol or other drugs give them intense pleasure and the sense that their needs are being satisfied. After they become addicted, they prefer the easy pleasure of their drug to the hard work of gaining and maintaining a friendly, loving sexual relationship. An ex-addict may make a good partner as long as he or she understands that you will not stick around if there is a relapse.

Successful long-term sex exists when love, friendship, and fun exist both in and out of bed. If this is not the case, one or both parties will have difficulty enjoying sex and the relationship will suffer. If love and fun are well satisfied, then even if the other needs are frustrated, sex may not suffer. If love and fun are not satisfied, then attempting to use the other needs—survival, power, and freedom—to keep the sex going will not work.

The sexual hormones, which are the result of our need to survive as a species, drive sex very strongly. In many female animals this is the only drive, and sex does not occur except when the hormones are active, when the female is in heat. In humans, both males and females are almost continually receptive and interested and, although the capacity may diminish, the urge continues from puberty.

But for their young to survive, higher animals need more than the sexual act. They need to care for both the child and the mother. This care is genetically driven. It is not love in the sense that we choose love, but it is the precursor to what eventually for us becomes the need for love and belonging.

No matter what society we live in, humans, almost all of whom have a normal need for love and belonging, are social beings as much or more than sexual beings. To satisfy our need for love and belonging, we have built marriage and family into all our societies. It is in our families that most of us as children learn that it is satisfying to care for each other. So when grown, we choose to repeat the process.

Unsocialized or poorly socialized humans are neither good lovers nor parents because they have not learned to love sufficiently and they frequently do not choose to care for their children. These people, especially males, frequently desire a lot of hormonal sex, but they are poor candidates for marriage. They may be sexual but they are not friendly and, because it is obvious that they have no idea what love is, they can be easily detected and avoided.

Men can satisfy their hormonal, sexual urges just by having sex. But for the species to survive, they have to go beyond sex and learn to love and care for their mates and children. So normal men, as well as women, are driven by a strong need for love and belonging. This need varies in strength from person to person. Some people (both men and women, but more men) have such a weak need for love that they never make the effort to learn how to satisfy it. This is a disastrous situation for marriage that I discuss in detail in the next chapter.

Since as humans we are conscious of what we are doing, almost all women who have a normal need for love and belonging and who grow up in a caring family learn to want loving sex much more than hormonal sex. When they engage in sex, they want the love and the security that a loving man can give them. They may engage in hormonal sex for a while, but if that is all there is, they grow uninterested.

If a woman who has a strong need for love marries a low-love man, the relationship will not be sexually satisfying, especially if he has a high need for survival and demands a lot of nonloving sex. To be fair, this also happens to men, but much less often. In low-love, high-survival people, hormonal sex continues to be a major drive all their lives and they are quite satisfied with a similar partner.

In the next chapter, I explain how to figure out your need-strength profile and that of your partner. It is from this profile that you can determine whether you are compatible in terms of the strength of your needs. From what I have explained so far, it is obvious that if one partner wants much more love and friendship than the other, sex will not be satisfactory.

If both partners can satisfy their need for love and friendship in their marriage and in their sexual relationship, they will have good long-term sex. I have briefly described friendship; it is now very important that I describe love that goes beyond friendship, what I call sexual love.

Sexual love occurs when men and women who are attracted to each other hormonally and begin to have sex discover that they like almost everything about each other as the person is *right now.* There is almost no "I would love you or love you more if . . . " Sexual love does not flourish in hopes for a return to the past or for a better future. It is a right-now, ongoing activity. If it does not work for several months, one or both parties lose interest and it is hard to recapture.

Sexual love is fragile. More than anything else, people fear rejection, and rejection of sexual love may be our strongest fear. It takes very little disappointment for us to begin to lose interest, and often we are afraid to tell our partner what we are disappointed about. We may go along in a relationship for years, dissatisfied with something, often minor, because we are afraid that if we bring it up we will be rejected or even ridiculed. What also stops us from asking is that we keep hoping our partner will figure out what we want so we don't have to ask. This rarely happens. We are better off asking, and I shortly suggest how to go about doing this.

Where sexual love is concerned, this reluctance to say what is bothering us is more the rule than the exception. Often it is the fear that what we want will be viewed as perverse in some way and the partner will be horrified and think he or she is living with someone abnormal. There are so many rules, both religious and societal, about what is and what is not proper sex that the fear of being seen as improper is always there. Partners who are successful sexually discover that there are no rules except as they want to make them. They talk it over and accept or reject what is requested and do it in a way that does not put the other down.

But usually what comes between the partners and spoils sex isn't even sexual. It may be using a crude expression to describe a woman or a man you see on the street or on TV or calling attention to someone's body in a way that offends the partner. It can be forgetting a common courtesey like saying "Please" or "Thank you" or "What would you like to do?" It may be how you eat, your cleanliness habits, being impatient, or even forgetting to put down the toilet seat that seriously diminishes a partner's interest in sex. Any perception, even very minor, of insensitivity to what the other wants may adversely affect sex.

All this adds up to one thing: *I can't accept you as you are and I want you to change.* More than anything else, hoping your partner will change or actively trying to change him or her destroys sexual love. That your dissatisfaction is justified makes no difference. You can be "right" and still kill your relationship. In practice, what this all adds up to is *criticism.* The criticism may be silent—a look, an inattention, a failure to do something—or it may be open and outspoken. But whatever it is, if your partner perceives it as criticism, your relationship is in trouble.

There is no such thing as constructive criticism. All criticism is destructive, and when it occurs in a relationship, it quickly kills sexual love. People with a strong need for power are often critical and they sometimes use clever put-downs. If you marry a critical person, expect this criticism.

For sexual love to last, couples must learn to deal with their dissatisfaction without criticism. If there is an axiom in the relations between the sexes, this is it. Criticism directed at a partner's sexual performance is the ultimate sexual turnoff. When I counsel dissatisfied couples, I always start by saying, "Whatever we say and do in this office, the rule is no criticism." Initially, I have to act like a boxing referee stepping in continually to break up the criticizing clinches that occur because the marriage has deteriorated to the point where criticism is almost the only means of communication. What I try to teach is how to express dissatisfaction without criticizing.

This is easy to understand but hard for people to put into practice. For many of us, it goes against a lifetime of lashing out critically or receiving criticism without being able to defend against it except by withdrawing. If the problem is not enough affection, a common cause of marital dissatisfaction, I suggest that the dissatisfied partner say, "I have a problem with the fact that there is not enough affection—kind words, hugs, kisses—in our relationship. I want you to help me figure out what I [not you!] can do to bring more affection into our lives." This is not criticism because it is not demanding that the other do anything different. It is saying help me to do something better than what *I* am doing now.

When done sincerely, using a listening and caring tone of voice, it tells the partner what is wrong in a way that asks the partner to help the dissatisfied one do better. It also says clearly that all problems are *our* problems; neither of us is perfect, but let's try to help each other work things out. It also says what is so basic to control theory: All each of us can do is control our own behavior; I can't control you and you can't control me, and I don't want to continue to waste time trying. Finally, it allows the partners to bring anything up because this is a totally nonrejecting way to approach a problem.

What happens frequently is that the partner says, "Well, I guess that I have been less affectionate because you have not done this or that and I got resentful because I didn't know how to tell you what was wrong without upsetting you." With a little judicious moderating and complimenting by the counselor, a lot can be done to help the relationship and to get the partners to understand that almost any disagreement or disappointment handled without criticism can increase sexual love. This often works, and if there is any love and friendship left, the marriage may be saved.

Withdrawing sex is the quickest and most hurtful way to express anger and, if the differences are not quickly patched up, the dissatisfaction becomes chronic. Both partners start to avoid sex, and loving sex disappears from the marriage or relationship. What is left—if the sex continues—is a kind of masturbation, which is rarely what is wanted.

In addition to helping people deal more effectively

with marital discord, this book teaches people who are thinking of starting a relationship how to avoid partners who may have genetically incompatible personalities. If you are already in a genetically discordant marriage, finding out where you are incompatible may give you a much better chance of dealing with this problem. To do this, I next look at the needs in terms of their strengths and how these strengths are reflected in our personalities.

5

Personality

Think of the people you know. Don't you identify them by a salient characteristic that defines their personality? Susan is loving. Jim is a macho bodybuilder. Janet is a compulsive spender. Henry is a cautious saver. Carol is a risk taker. Harold is a ladies man. Pauline is a born teacher. . . . The list could go on and on. It is my contention that these identifying characteristics are strongly connected to the pattern or profile of the strength of our needs.

In the above examples, Jim, who works out a lot by himself, needs a lot of power and freedom. And since there are not many laughs in a lonely workout, fun and belonging are less necessary for him. Pauline is almost the opposite. She is attracted to teaching by strong needs for fun and love. She is the authority in the classroom so she has a moderate need for power. In addition, restricted as she is to the classroom, it is appropriate that she is endowed with no more than an average need for freedom.

There is no way to predict how people will choose to satisfy their needs. What we can predict is that what they choose will fit their need-strength profile. Jim could have chosen to become a high-powered defense lawyer with few friends who seeks fame but who works all the time. Good-humored and upbeat Pauline could have chosen to be a nurse or social worker. What this chapter explains is that all of us have need-strength profiles that lead us to create a personality, and from that personality a way of life that fits this profile. For example, if I have a strong need for love, I will seek love in one of its many varieties; I will never lead the life of a loner.

The more we are aware of our need-strength profile, the more we will be able to figure out with whom we are likely to be compatible. Jim, with a strong need for power and freedom, might marry Pauline, who has a strong need for love and fun, because both might have a strong need for survival and might be strongly sexually attracted to each other. But once married, they will find little to talk about and may not even be able to become good friends. After a while, with familiarity and not much love, the sexual attraction will diminish, and when it does, the marriage will be in trouble. If they know before marriage that their profiles are so different, they may hesitate, or at least become aware of what they need to work on if they go ahead.

The most common complaint of one or both partners

in a relationship is, "I can't live with him (or her) the way she (or he) is. He (or she) has to change if this marriage is to work." What we are not aware of is how the strength of our needs has led us to be the way we are, and so we tend to believe we are far more flexible than we actually are. We don't realize that once we settle into a reasonably satisfying life that fits the strength of our needs, we find it almost impossible to make a major change. By major, I mean something new that is not satisfying to our need-strength profile, for example, to go from a moderate to a passionate lover. Therefore, in this chapter I attempt to teach you how to figure out your own need-strength profile, and also the need-strength profile of your partner if he or she is unwilling to do this with you. If we are to get along well with those we live with, this is vital information.

If you are in the beginning stages of a relationship, this is the time to make this assessment. Find out early if you are well matched and also become aware of where there is potential for trouble. Then you can try to deal with some of the differences before you get married and also learn how to deal with any differences that arise after marriage.

If you are in an unsatisfying relationship, you already know that you have problems. What you do not know is if the problems are based on a big difference in the strength of your needs or are a result of life choices. How you are choosing to live is more easily changed than your need-strength profiles. But even if your profiles are in conflict, knowing where and what these differences are gives you information that may enable you to solve the problem. For example, you can build on your compatibility and attempt to avoid areas where you are incompatible.

If Jim were married to Pauline and the marriage became unsatisfying and he wanted to do something about it, he could demonstrate his workout skills in her class, which might fulfill his need for power. Pauline might become more tolerant of the time Jim spent working out, since he used his skills to help her, and thus she might allow him the freedom he needs so much. Given the freedom, he might become more loving as he appreciates her tolerance.

Marriage is difficult; just a little help can mean the difference between a fair and a good marriage. Even this small effort toward more compatibility isn't easy, but it is their best chance. Pauline is not going to give up teaching and caring for her students; Jim is not going to give up working out by himself. They need to find a bridge between these very different lifestyles.

To illustrate the need-strength profile, I use myself as an example and assess the strength of my needs on a scale of 1 to 5: 1 = very weak, 2 = below average, 3 = average, 4 = above average, 5 = very strong. Then I put these individual assessments together in the order of survival, love and belonging, power, freedom, and fun to build my own need-strength profile. I explain how my personality is the result of that profile. Next I compare my profile with the profile of my late wife to show clearly how to use these profiles to figure out compatibility. Finally, I explain that certain need-strength profiles are predictive of success in marriage and others are predictive of failure. Be cautious if you enter into a relationship with someone in the latter group.

The Strength of My Needs

Survival—3, Average

As I assess my life from the standpoint of this need, I am much more of a saver than a spender, but I am not acquisitive and get no particular satisfaction out of what money can buy. I am not a health fanatic, but I am careful about my health and I eat sensibly. I continue to have a strong interest in sex as I approach my seventieth year, and that has something to do with at least an average need to survive. On the other hand, I know that I am not above average in needing to survive because I am not willing to settle for the status quo in any part of my life. In fact, all my life I have been eager to take risks and to explore new experiences and new ideas. Putting this together, I think I am well within the average range where survival is concerned.

Love and Belonging—4, Above Average

I am very much in need of personal love and intimacy and I am very concerned about the welfare of my fellow human beings. Most of my time is spent in an effort to create more satisfying schools for teachers and children. On the other hand, I have no need to socialize with strangers; for example, I rarely talk or try to get acquainted with people who sit next to me on airplanes even though I fly continually. It is this reluctance to reach out to people I don't know coupled with my strong need for closeness to those I love or know well that makes me think that I am above average but not at the top in the strength of this need.

Power—4, Above Average

There is no doubt that I want very much to excel in my field and get recognition or I wouldn't be writing this book. But even in my field, although I crave recognition, I do not crave personal power. I don't like to give orders or tell people what to do for the sake of being in charge. For example, I head a large organization but I serve it far more than I run it and I am always looking for ways to support my people and to encourage them to develop new ideas. I delegate the operation to trusted associates; I listen to what they have to say and I almost always agree.

I make a very good living and I want to be more than financially secure; I don't want to have to think about money at all. In a small way, I try to plow some of what I earn back into helping people use my ideas and I never let anyone who sponsors my presentations lose money, which also gives me a sense of power. I do not understand people who take from the needy, who lay off people when their company is reaping large profits, and I have no comprehension of people whose salaries are in the tens of millions. Even if they later give to charity, I think of how much better the lives of many people they employed could have been if they had taken less and used their skills to do more for those whose work helped them achieve success.

In my relationships with women I am not at all competitive. In my organization, women have an equal chance for whatever power is available and have availed themselves of this opportunity. I want to be recognized as one of the top people in not only my initial field, psychiatry, but also in education and management. To get there, I make an intense effort to persuade people to use my ideas, but I never try to force them to do so. I see myself as a leader, not a boss. This adds up to my being above average but not at the top where the strength of the power need is concerned.

Freedom—5, Very Strong

More than anything else this need dominates my life. I listen to people very carefully but I can't stand it when people try to tell me how to live my life, or worse, try to make me do things I do not want to do. I am very fortunate that I have been successful and have been able to choose almost all I do. For the unsuccessful, unfortunately, there is little freedom anywhere. I am a firm believer that people should not try to tell other people how to live: There are no experts, including psychiatrists, here.

This book is dedicated to telling you what I believe you need to know about how we function as human beings. But it is not dedicated to telling you specifically what to do with this knowledge: It is up to you to figure this out. The most I do is make suggestions based on my knowledge and experience. This is the way I have lived my whole life, including the therapy I have pioneered, reality therapy. Therapists are teachers, not tellers. As I passionately love to learn and use what I learn, I want others to do the same. I am a strong believer in freedom of opportunity and the pursuit of happiness.

At the same time, I believe in responsibility. No one has the right to be free to do what he or she likes at the expense of another human, even another creature. If we don't take more responsibility for what we do to satisfy our needs, especially our need for power, we will soon become an endangered species.

Finally, it is difficult to reconcile my need for freedom and the restrictions of marriage. My late wife and I had many discussions about this, especially the conflict between my obligations to her and our family and my desire to pursue my career. The compromise was that she helped me, not just because she loved me, but because she believed in what I was trying to do. But to get this compromise, we had to talk and listen to each other, and it was never easy. I envy married people who have a lesser need for freedom; their lives seem so much easier.

Fun—5, Very Strong

As much as freedom, I love fun. I like to laugh and joke. I strongly dislike seriousness if it is at all pretentious. I feel sorry for people who seem to have no sense of humor, but, for me, the humor has to make a point. Unless I can learn or teach from it, it is pointless.

As explained, I firmly believe from personal experience that fun is the reward for learning, and I have learned the most by far from people who are able to drive their points or experiences home with humor. I think the strongest people are those who are able to laugh at themselves. An inability to do this signifies a lack of balance in the personality, too much of a desire for power, too little for fun. Power-driven people like to make jokes at the expense of others but they are not fun-loving; they are power-hungry put-downers.

Fortunately, I am not so driven by power that I need power recreation. I like to play games and I like to win, but I do not have to win all the time. I get genuine pleasure when my opponent makes a good shot or the team I am rooting against makes a superb play. I like reading, travel, theater, art, music, and nonviolent movies, so I have no difficulty finding things to do that most educated, well-read women enjoy.

Creating the Need-Strength Profile

All the need-strength profiles in this book show the strength of each need in this order: survival, love and belonging, power, freedom, and fun. Based on what I have just described about myself, which tells a lot about my personality, this is how I arrive at my need-strength profile. I am average in survival (3); above average in love (4); above average in power (4); very needful of both freedom (5) and fun (5). Therefore, in the order of the needs as listed above, my need-strength profile is 34455. It is from this 34455 profile that I have created the personality I have just attempted to describe.

Knowing what my profile is can be useful to me in many ways. First I use it to see where it was compatible and incompatible with the need-strength profile of Naomi, my late wife. To begin, I think it is fair to say that our marriage of forty-six years was a good one. Mostly we were loving and considerate of each other and neither of us ever thought seriously about divorce. We did have disagreements, mostly over my need for freedom, but we talked these over, sometimes heatedly but almost never to the point of fighting. That we were able to find many things to do together that we both enjoyed allowed us to get over our differences easily in almost all cases. To have a marriage that lasted that long, we must have had compatible profiles. Naomi was below average in survival (2); even stronger than me in love and belonging (5); similar in power (4); average in freedom (3); and above average in fun (4). This makes her profile 25434 compared to my 34455.

Comparing Our Need-Strength Profiles

Survival—Hers 2, Mine 3

Because Naomi had less of a survival need than I have, she had less of a need to save. It was not much less, but over the years I had to learn to be less of a tightwad. We worked it out by my acceding to her, and I never regretted it. Indeed, I knew she was right, but the need-strength difference was always there and I always felt momentary tugs of discomfort, for example, when she told me we were going to fly first class when we went overseas. I was, however, not so uncomfortable that I did not enjoy first class, so my need for survival was not above average. If it had been a 4 or 5, we might have had some real dissension.

Love—Hers 5, Mine 4

Her need for love and belonging was greater than mine, but not by too much, so we were able to satisfy each other's needs most of the time. Where we differed is that she had a greater need for family beyond our personal family. Also, she was much more inclined to make new acquaintances and to strike up casual conversations. I did not resent that at all; in fact, I enjoyed her friendliness as long as she did not insist, which she never did, that I be like her. I also appreciated her social skills, which were very useful in the work we did together.

Power—Hers 4, Mine 4

Our power needs were both above average but, again, we had little conflict. She shared much of my work and helped me to write, for which I gave her much credit, so most of the time there were few power problems. She always cautioned me that I might be reaching too far. But at the same time she joined me in what I was doing, and since things usually worked out, there was no problem. We were never competitive, which is the key to marital success when both partners have strong power needs.

Freedom—Hers 3, Mine 5

Our biggest problems, as I mentioned, were with freedom. I have a very strong need for freedom, and hers was average. She could not understand why I wanted to do all that I did by myself, especially to create so many ideas and to work away from home so much. We never did resolve this problem, but gradually she accepted that this is the way I am. It became easier for her when the children were grown and she was not as burdened with their care. But we recognized early that this was a great difference; we respected that difference and worked on it in many ways.

She accepted me the way I am. We argued once in a while and she complained a lot, but she didn't try to change me; she recognized that this was impossible. I did as much as I could—never enough—to satisfy her complaints and she appreciated what I did. The need differences made things difficult, but they never threatened our marriage and we rarely withdrew love from each other.

A strong need for freedom on the part of one partner is a red flag to any relationship, and the couple had better recognize this early and work on it continually. Marriages where one or both partners crave freedom work better when both partners also have a low need for power (we didn't, thus the arguments and complaints) and a very high need for love and fun (we were close here). The joys of all the love and fun coupled with a low need for power, which means not much desire to change the other, might make a high-freedom marriage work better than ours.

Fun—Hers 4, Mine 5

There was a small problem with fun, but it was never excessive. Naomi had some trouble figuring out why I was always getting involved with new ideas, why I didn't settle down with the success I had achieved. To me that would have been boring; I need new learning and new activities—creativity is so much fun. We shared enough fun activities—travel and the theater—so that my pursuit of new ideas did not become a problem. Besides, she always laughed at my jokes and wisecracks and that worked well for both of us.

Robert and Francesca

Since their lives have been made so public, I think it would be fun to compare the need-strength profiles of the fictional lovers in *The Bridges of Madison County* to try to see what went wrong. Wrong, that is, if you are a romantic who was hoping for a happier ending. I would say that Robert was average in survival, love, and power (3,3,3), had a very high need for freedom (5), and a moderate need for fun (3), giving him a 33353 profile. I base this on the fact that he never remarried and was highly competent but not passionate about the life he led—except that it gave him the chance to be free, his great passion. Since there was not much time for fun in the short relationship, I am guessing that his need for fun was average.

Francesca had a high need for survival (5) or she

might have pursued Robert, coupled with a high need for love (5) or she would never have considered doing what she did so passionately. But it was this same high need for love that made her so reluctant to leave her children and a good, if unexciting, husband. Her power and freedom needs were low (2,2) or she would not have stayed so long, without complaints, in a passionless marriage. Again, I am not able to assess her need for fun, but it was probably low (2), as she did not have the ability to even want to try anything that would require learning. Altogether her profile was 55222.

As much as Robert was able to love Francesca, he was no Lochinvar. He rode off on his horse alone, even though none of her "kinsmen" would have been in hot pursuit if he had taken her with him. If she had pursued him, he would have been kind. But with his average love and high freedom needs, he did not have the long-term capacity to love her the way she would have wanted to be loved if she had been willing to make the sacrifice to go with him. And I think she recognized this. Her survival and love needs kept her loyal and, as she was not driven by a strong need for power or freedom, she let him go. It was a sad but not a tragic parting, and I don't think they could have sustained very long in a licit relationship what was so illicitly wonderful for a week.

If you have read their story, do your own Robert and Francesca need-strength profiles and see what you come up with. There is no right or wrong; it is just a good exercise to prepare you for figuring out your and your mate's need-strength profiles.

Need-Strength Profiles That Are Good for Marriage

Last night, I had dinner with a couple who are among my oldest friends. Knowing that they have had a good marriage for forty-four years and believing that they would be more than willing, I asked them if with my help they would construct their own need-strength profiles. They had a lot of fun doing this and took it very seriously. It turned out that his is 45235; hers 25335. As we discussed the similarities and differences, it became clear that the only incompatibility in their marriage (very minor) that has led to some negotiation is survival. She is a risk taker and he is very conservative. Not a big deal, but they agreed that their profiles showed this quite clearly.

I mention this here because one aspect of their profiles, very different from my marriage, is very interesting. His power need (2) is lower than hers (3). Of all the compatibilities that lead to a good marriage, this couple has them both: they share high love and low power. Sharing a strong need for love is always good, but coupled with the tolerance of each other that accompanies low power needs on the part of both partners, this pattern is highly predictive of marital success. As men have more access to power, his lower need for it makes him a very satisfied man, and her higher but not too high need makes their marriage equal instead of competitive. And as we discussed their profiles afterward, this is exactly what they had discovered in their happy marriage.

It is also obvious that it is good if both have the same

survival needs. In this case, that was their only difficulty, minor because they are comfortable economically. Nevertheless, it is better if both are spenders or savers, both risk takers or conservative. Anytime there is a large difference in this need, there is potential trouble.

That love needs should both be high is obvious, and I have explained how desirable it is if both have a low need for power. It is also good when one has a high need for power and the other has a low need, so that the bossy is less opposed by the bossed one.

In Naomi's and my case, with both of us having a fairly high need for power (both 4), we could have easily run into difficulty if we had not recognized this and worked together to gain the power we both needed. Many couples are not willing or able to do this. If the man is employed in a job where there is little that the wife can do to get involved, and she is in the same situation, there can be severe difficulties as each struggles for power separately and even in competition with each other. As long as each is able to satisfy his or her power needs at work, there may be little difficulty at home. But if one or both are unable to satisfy a high power need at work, as is frequently the case, there is always potential for trouble at home.

Or if the high-power wife tries—it is worse if her husband coerces her to do this—to stay home and take care of the house while her husband is out in the world satisfying his need for power, the marriage suffers. As much as taking care of children is satisfying to survival, love, and fun, most women do not find it satisfying to their need for power no matter how hard they try. Women with a high need for power are better off working and much better off if their husbands support them in this endeavor by doing their part with child care. It is clear that the power need is more complicated than the love or survival need for a good marriage. Equal power, for example, works best when the need is low for both partners.

If both partners have low or average freedom needs, this too is best for marriage. High freedom on the part of both works if it is balanced by needing a lot of love and no more than average power. The high love keeps them together; the low power keeps them from trying to restrict each other's freedom. Still, my guess is that this is a chancy marriage; high freedom is always in opposition to any restrictive relationship and marriage is restrictive.

If one partner has a high need for freedom and the other a low or moderate need for freedom, there is, as in my case, resentment on the part of the lower-need partner. We had high love, which made this disparity livable, but it would have been better for the marriage if Naomi also had a low power need. This was not the case and so we had some trouble. Still, there is one saving grace for such a marriage or even for a marriage when both have high freedom needs: people with a high need for freedom also seem to be creative. Creativity thrives on freedom, so if the high-freedom partner, or partners, is given some space, the resulting creativity can be very good for the marriage. (I discuss the importance of creativity in chapter 8.)

Fun is also tied to creativity, and high-fun people who are able to satisfy this need in marriage tend to be highly creative. Marriages are strengthened when both partners have high fun needs. If they share even average fun needs this is good; and if they share low fun needs this is not harmful to the marriage (although they will never know what they are missing). But a disparity in the need for fun is bad for marriage, and the fun partner looks for others to laugh with.

The saving grace is that high-fun people are not usually attracted to low-fun people. If you have a high fun need and you are not married, don't settle for anyone less than average in this need, and the higher the better. It is not a need that someone can hide, so the strength of the fun need is easy to assess. Let's now take a look at the opposite side of the coin.

Need-Strength Profiles That Are Bad for Marriage

Based on many years of experience working with a variety of people who were in pain and dissatisfied with their lives, I have concluded that some need-strength profiles are bad for marriage. The profile that always bodes badly for marriage is 11555. This is much more common in men than women. If a woman with a more average profile, such as one around 33333, marries a man with a profile even close to 11555, she is reserving a place for herself in hell.

It is the low, almost absent, need for love and the very high need for power that is the crucial antimarriage part of this configuration. This is because 11555 is the classic profile of a sociopath or psychopath, a person who cares only about his own satisfaction, even at the expense of risking his life as indicated by his low need for survival.

But almost equally bad for marriage is a person who has an average or even high need for survival coupled with low love, high power, and not much need for fun, the extreme of which is 51531. Women may have that profile, but it is rare because they almost never have the low-love, high-power ratio (X15XX). One woman most of us "know," Scarlett O'Hara, comes close to this profile—I would give her a 52542. She was very high in survival, low in love (she didn't grieve too much for her daughter), high in power and freedom (she insisted on having things her way), and low in fun (Scarlett was no bundle of joy).

I would give Rhett Butler a 25455 profile. He was below average in survival (he took risks easily), high in love, high but not as high as Scarlett in power, and very high in freedom and fun (these are obvious). It is easy to see that in their marriage the crucial differences were in survival, love, and fun, and differences as large as these are usually not reconcilable, as theirs were not.

Men who have the sociopathic profile, 11555, have no difficulty attracting women because they seem to be so strong, and their disregard for convention is so prevalent that their high freedom and low survival needs allow them to be very seductive. And until they begin to exploit this attractiveness—it usually takes no longer than a few weeks—they are a lot of fun.

They can be exciting lovers, but their love is all for

exploitation without real feeling. It is because there is so little feeling that they can be so loving. They also can love so easily because, with a low need for survival, they have no concern about providing a future. They live for the moment. Because the future never crosses their minds, they are not deterred by the threat of punishment.

These men are easily recognized because they almost always have a track record of going from victim to victim, promising love but delivering abuse and exploitation. If the woman is suspicious, their appealing pitch to a new victim is, "With you I am going to be different." Women fall for that line time and time again, but these men are never different. With a high need for power and a low or nonexistent need for love, they do not have the capacity to act differently.

The way to recognize these supercharming men is that they have a history and it is all bad. Ask them. If they are evasive, beware. If they tell you the truth, which they may while in the same breath promising that they will change for you, run as fast as you can. They are unreliable, always full of excuses, borrow money and even steal from you, and usually drink and use drugs. There is always an excuse, a "good" reason, and it all seems so plausible because they are so expert at what they do. If you meet a man who seems supercharming, ask yourself why such a charmer is available and attracted to you. Anyone who seems too good to be true usually is.

Another group of people, again mostly men, who are not good for marriage—unless you want to take care of them—have a profile similar to 25113. This is the mama's boy, the very dependent person who can barely survive without help. He has a lot of love but, with no need for power, he cannot back up that love with action or effort. His need for freedom is low; he is satisfied if someone takes care of him. He is not usually abusive, but he can be if he is not taken care of. His need for fun is average, but again, if taken care of, he can be an enjoyable companion.

The best way to detect these men is that they hang around but they don't do much. They either don't work or have trouble holding a job. They are great planners—it is all going to happen soon—but they don't carry out their plans. They, too, are full of excuses, endlessly explaining that what went wrong was someone else's fault. For them the grass is always greener on the other side, but unless you lift them, they never get over the fence.

In general, what to look out for in both women and men, but in my experience mostly men, are those who have a wide variation between their needs, with love being the low-strength need. Anyone with a low need for love and high need for one or more of survival, power, and freedom is a poor candidate for marriage. I have explained the profile of a low-love/high-power man. A low-love/high-freedom man (31353) is similar except he rarely marries or, if he does, he is around for such a short time that the marriage becomes incidental.

There is also a problem, again usually with men, with a low-love/high-survival partner who also has a low need for fun (51331). This man works hard, is a good provider, and is not abusive, but there is no joy and very little loving sex in the marriage. He may demand a lot of sex based on his large supply of survival hormones, but that is hardly satisfying to a woman who needs love. Almost all women can easily tell the difference between hormonal sex—some call it hit-and-run sex—and loving sex.

If you are married to such a man, everyone tells you how lucky you are: "He is such a good provider." But if you want companionship, you are far from lucky. If, however, you have about the same profile, you may get along, which is about all you can expect. With this profile he will help you take good care of the children, which may be the main strength and bond of the marriage. That's not bad; the children do well and may not inherit his extreme need-strength profile.

I have already discussed the dependent person who has a high need for love and a low need for power and usually a low need for freedom. But how about a mate with an average need for survival, love, power, and freedom but a very low need for fun (33331)? This is not a disastrous combination, but if you have a normal or higher need for fun, you are going to have to seek it outside the marriage. What fun you get on your wedding day is what you will have for the rest of your life. This mate is not going to learn anything new and will become a world-class television watcher.

So far, I have focused mostly on men because I have found that men find it far more difficult than women to adjust to the demands of marriage. They tend to have higher needs for power and freedom. This is probably based on the fact that women are the biological rearers of children, so women evolved with more love and survival genes than men. Men certainly cooperated, but they had to wander to hunt while the woman gathered, which led to men being self-sufficient.

Since the most powerful men tended to survive and leave more descendents, their sons inherited their genes and the common male need-strength profile is the result. The women these men found desirable had high survival, high love, low power, and low freedom needs—they stayed home, reared the children, and didn't complain. They passed these genes along to their daughters, leading to the common female need-strength profile. Men who got more of their mother's genes were less competitive and left fewer descendents, as did women who got more of their father's genes. Thus the more common need-strength profiles, which is how evolution works.

As we have moved into civilization this difference has become less extreme. There are, however, plenty of men who are high in love and women who are high in power, so it is best to assess the people you meet and hold out for a compatible profile rather than to settle for any evolutionary average. As far as fun is concerned, men had the biggest payoff for new ideas in male-dominated societies, but women had to be clever to survive and take care of children, so the fun genes developed equally and I do not see any strong evolutionary difference in respect to fun between men and woman.

Men with average profiles like 33333 or even 34333 do badly married to women with significantly lower needs for love than they have. Poor marriage profiles in women are 31543 and, even worse, 31553. The latter is a great woman to be in business with or to employ in a nonpeople business, but not a good person to marry if you are a man with an average or above average need for love.

For a successful marriage, a loving man needs a loving woman more than a loving woman needs a loving man because, in our culture and almost all others, men do not have as much ability as women to find satisfying, nonsexual love and belonging with family or friends. Thus, women married to less loving men find it easier to compensate for a lower love need in their mate than men do.

Men who have an average or above average need for love, when married to women whose need for love is below average, often compensate by engaging in affairs rather than ending the marriage because women with profiles like 41553 are often highly competent mates in all other respects. Of course, this is not always the reason for men's affairs, but it is a common cause. People who have affairs, both men and women, are looking for more than sex; they are looking for sexual love, and when they find it, the affair tends to last.

Finally, here is a possible need-profile for child or wife abusers. They have an extreme profile, such as 51533. It is the first three numbers, 515, that are crucial; the last two numbers are less important. The child or wife abuser has a strong hormonal need for sex as shown by the very high need for survival, an abnormally low need for love, and a very high need for power.

To satisfy this abnormal pattern, these men select powerless people like children or women, whom they can dominate and with whom they try to satisfy their need for power and sex. Abusive husbands and fathers frequently rationalize their behavior by saying that they really love the child or woman but they had to teach obedience, and our male-dominated society does not hold them as responsible as it should for these rationalizations. The difference between them and psychopaths is that the psychopath usually does not have the strong need for survival, often risks his life, and is not nearly as dominated by sexual urges.

The Marriage Prediction Experiment

The point of this chapter is to teach you how need-strength profiles can help you understand your own and others' personalities. If you can do this, you have a better than average chance to select a compatible mate or to work out problems in your marriage that are caused by disparate profiles. The first impetus for this book was the following experiment.

Several years ago at a large meeting I had a chance to do an experiment with about 200 of my colleagues, all of whom were familiar with control theory. To begin, I explained what I have just explained in this chapter, but in much less detail, and told them to break into groups of four or five. Then I asked them to write out the need-strength profiles of both their mother and father, rating each need as weak, average, or strong. (I used a three-step strength scale instead of the five-step scale I use now, but I don't believe that this small change made any significant difference in the outcome of the experiment.)

Then on a separate piece of paper I asked them to rate the success of their parents' marriage: 3 for a good marriage, 2 for average, and 1 for a poor or broken marriage. Next I told them to show these mother-father profiles to all the other members of the group. After I gave all the participants some of the information that I have just explained about which profiles are compatible and which are not, I asked each of the other participants to rate the marriages as good, average, or poor on the basis of these profiles. When all members of the group finished, they compared their estimates with those of the children of the rated marriages.

I then asked who had rated the marriages accurately, just from seeing these need-strength profiles and knowing nothing else about the marriages. The results were far better than I anticipated. Almost 95 percent of the people were able to rate the marriages accurately based only on the profiles of the couples, which shows that it is possible to construct accurate need-strength profiles for people you know well and that these profiles can serve as a powerful predictive instrument for the success of a marriage.

If your marriage is less satisfying than you would like, I encourage you to do this for your own marriage with or without your mate. You might, just for practice, ask some friends whose parents you know and who know your parents to join you in constructing a need-strength profile of your parents and their parents to see if you agree on what you have constructed. Talk it over and do it for other couples you both know also. Exercises like these will help you learn to construct accurate need-strength profiles.

The profiles of you and your mate can show you where you may be seriously incompatible. You can use this warning to deal with differences in the strength of your needs before problems get out of hand. This takes strength and courage, and some couples, especially early in marriage, may find this approach unromantic. But a bad marriage is more than unromantic—it is hell.

Assessing Your Own and Others' Need-Strength Profiles

I have provided a lot of information that you can use to construct your own need profile and profiles of others you know, especially your partner. Like most of us, your needs are probably close to average in strength, with the numbers ranging from 2 to 4. It is certainly possible that you will have some very strong or very weak needs, but it is unlikely that your needs will be as different in strength as the needs of the antisocial people just discussed, with a very low need for love and a very high need for power.

More likely, if you have some 4 or 5 needs, as I do, they are not joined by any 1 or 2 needs, especially if your life is productive and you have had or are still having good relationships. Do the ratings several times, because as you think about it, you will come up with new perspectives on yourself and use them to refine your profiles. Remember, there is no right or wrong answer.

If your partner is willing, ask him or her to figure out a need-strength profile. Your partner can do this openly with you or in private. Initially, you are looking for accuracy, not self-disclosure. If your partner will not do this, put yourself in your partner's shoes and rate him or her as best as you can. You will be amazingly accurate.

After you become aware of your own and your partner's need-strength profiles, you need to use this information in more depth than I have talked about. Therefore, I now move from the needs and their strength, which are general, to the actual people, things, and beliefs that best satisfy these needs that we store in what I believe is the core of our life: our quality world.

6

The Quality World

Starting shortly after birth, all of our behavior is an attempt to achieve whatever we want at the time. We spend all our lives learning what best satisfies our needs and we store this knowledge in a part of our memory that I call our quality world. Specifically, we learn that certain people, things, and beliefs are highly satisfying to one or more of our five needs, and it is this need-satisfying knowledge that dominates our lives. In a relationship, we always create a picture in our quality world of what we want that relationship to be. We create a picture of how we want to be treated and how we will try to treat our partner so that both of us will feel good and want to continue in that relationship.

The process that creates our quality world begins when, as babies, we put our mother's picture into the beginning of these worlds. Initially, driven by the pain of unsatisfied needs, all a baby can do is cry. Assuming it is being cared for by its mother—she cares for it because it is usually the most important picture in her quality world—the baby very soon begins to learn that when it is uncomfortable and cries, something good happens. The pain stops and is replaced by a much better feeling. Very shortly, it learns that this marvellous, consistently pain-relieving, pleasure-producing entity is its mother, and it stores this vital knowledge in its quality world, usually as a picture, where in most cases this "mother picture" remains for the rest of its life.

As we live, we learn and remember almost countless things, but very little of what we learn and remember is stored in our quality world. This is because only a tiny amount of what we learn is satisfying enough to warrant, as our mother was, entry into our quality world. Even when we are grown, this world is very small. It contains only the most satisfying examples of what we know.

Very early we put ourselves in this world, picturing ourselves with all the need-satisfying accomplishments we hope we can achieve as well as how we want to be treated by others. Besides ourselves, we put in our loved ones, our closest friends, our prized possessions and what we would like to possess or visit, and our cherished ideas and ideals such as religious beliefs. These are the people, things, and ideas that we have found to be most satisfying to one or more of our basic needs.

It is our quality world, therefore, that is the instrument of our falling in love. Sometime, early in our adolescence, driven strongly but not exclusively by the sex hormones that are generated by our need to survive as a species, we begin to form an idea of who would make an ideal mate and, from this early idea, a picture of this person begins to take shape in our quality world. For boys it may be a picture with some of the qualities of their mother; for girls, their father. But driven by the popular media, we also begin to add to this ideal picture based on characters from movies, television, magazines, and books, as well as relatives, neighbors, teachers, and friends. For almost all of us, this romanticizing continues most of our lives and sets the stage for the universal process of "falling" in love.

Unfortunately, for many of us this picture is highly idealized or romanticized and bears little resemblance to who actually is available to marry. In marriage, "the honeymoon is over" is the pop phrase for the difference between the idealized person we hope is our mate and the person who, shortly after marriage, we "discover" is our mate. What we can learn from control theory is to take a good look at the picture we have formed in our head of the "idealized" mate and try to figure out if this picture is reasonably close to the reality of who is available.

Most of us are aware that the quality world picture of our mate is not realistic, and many of us are able to recognize that the person we are falling in love with hardly fits that picture. Still, too many of us delude ourselves into believing that given our love, our prospective partner will change in the direction of the picture of him or her that we have placed in our quality world. More human misery is caused by the shattering of this delusion than anything else we experience.

Although mates do change, in most instances they change in a direction far different from what we want. As we try to control our mates so that they become closer to what we want, we usually do not take into account the strength of their needs and the pictures of what they want. We tend to be blinded by what we want and continue to try to force them to change. The most common way to try to control our mate is to withdraw love and attention. As we do this, our mate finds less satisfaction in the relationship and withdraws love in return. Instead of getting closer, the couple grows farther apart.

In many cases, the marriage "stabilizes" at some distance from what one or both want—usually farther from what they had before each tried to remake the other— because one or both recognize that things are getting worse and they stop trying. This stabilized, less happy or even unhappy, marriage becomes their way of life. In many instances, it does not stabilize, and instead ends in divorce.

Some people learn from their divorce to take a much closer look at their own quality world and the quality world of a new partner before they get remarried, and the second or third marriage is more successful. Many, however, do not learn from this failure and persist in the same delusional pattern. For example, there are countless instances of women (it is usually women) marrying several alcoholics.

To prevent this common, miserable process, we need to learn much more about our quality worlds and then build a quality world that is based on self-knowledge and reality. If we can do this initially, we have a good chance

for a satisfying first marriage; if we do it later, for a satisfying subsequent relationship. If we cannot do this, we
have little or no chance for a good marriage.

The first thing to learn about your quality world is
that it is yours. You decide what to put into it and what
to take out of it. No one can make you love him or her.
For my own selfish desires, I may be able to figure out
and then tell you all the things you want to hear, but I
can't make you believe them. I may, however, know that
you want to believe me very much, and I can exploit that
knowledge, but it is still up to you to put me into your
quality world as a potential mate.

But if you do not know anything about your quality
world, you have no way of knowing that no matter what
I may tell you, it is still you who must make the decision
to put me into your quality world. In the end, it is you,
not me, who made me into the person who seems to be
the epitome of what you want. Once you put me into
your quality world, even if you created a very unrealistic
picture of me, you will be reluctant to take that picture
out. You have convinced yourself that I am the person
with whom you can best satisfy your needs. In short, you
love me.

If you were to remove me, you fear you would have
to settle for less satisfaction than you want. So as I tell
you more and more of what you want to hear, you make
no effort to create a more realistic picture. In actual practice, for a long time, usually years, difficult as I may be
and far different as I am from what you thought I was
initially, I am all you choose to have. If you take me out
of your quality world, you have no one, only an empti-

ness. This void is so frightening that you stick with me, miserable as we both are. You don't know that you can change what you want to a more realistic picture. And even if you did, you have invested so much time and energy in me that you don't believe you have the strength to go through this difficult process again.

So you, like millions of others, settle for misery—misery you might have avoided if you had known more about the quality world in the beginning or misery you can now avoid by using this knowledge to start over. We all need to understand this psychological process; it is the core of our lives.

We must learn to be very careful about who we put into our quality world. And if we make a mistake, we must learn to change what is in this world if we are to get what we want. We also need to learn how to appraise the quality world of the person we are having so much difficulty relating to now and see if it is possible for us to love a person with that quality world. And if we give this person up, we must use what we have learned to appraise the quality world of someone new and then see if we can actually find a compatible place for this new person in our quality world. We cannot expect that person to change his or her world; we must find someone who has a quality world with which we can live and grow.

Learning to Create and Change Pictures

Even if you know nothing about control theory, if you are involved in a long-term, happy marriage, the picture you have created in your quality world of yourself is accurate. The picture of your mate is accurate. And the picture of your marriage, based on compatible pictures of the way you want to live, is accurate. But if you are among the millions of unhappily married people, then one or more of those three pictures is unrealistic and must be changed if you are to have a chance for a happy marriage.

There is no shortcut or easy way to create a realistic picture of yourself in your quality world. Since this picture is the way you want things to be, it tends to be idealized. To some extent this is good; it gives you the impetus to move your life beyond where it is, to dream, create, and constantly improve. But if it is too far divorced from reality, it sets up unrealistic expectations that you cannot satisfy and, in trying to do so, you may destroy your chances for happiness.

The best way that I can teach you to create a realistic picture of yourself in your quality world is to continue what I started in the previous chapter and explain how I believe I created the quality world that I am living with at this time. After my wife died, and after a reasonable period of mourning, I decided I did not want to be lonely anymore, so I was faced with the difficult problem of trying to find a new long-term relationship.

At age sixty-eight, I had a long history, a lot of experience, and a great deal of knowledge about how human beings function. Still, I was not prepared for how difficult it is to find someone new. To begin, I did a lot of thinking about the picture I have of myself right now in my quality world. And I thought about what I, with this picture, can bring to a new relationship. Next, I had to figure out what kind of a woman I should create in my quality world who would be compatible both with me and my present picture of a new long-term relationship. All the while, I was aware that I was driven by loneliness, so I had to be careful neither to idealize myself, which means my capacity to bring love to the relationship, nor the person with whom I might attempt to become involved, nor the relationship we would try to create.

The easiest way to figure out the pictures of who I am, who I want, and what would be a satisfying relationship with that woman is to expand on my personality as I explained it earlier. I described myself as having a 34455 personality, average in survival, above average in love and power, and very high in freedom and fun. Here I attempt to describe the pictures I have created in my quality world that are compatible with that personality.

I wrote this before I became deeply involved with Carleen and before I saw her description of her quality world, which comes next. As you will see when you read what we both wrote, we are very compatible and this compatibility has increased. As I tried to put myself into the shoes of someone in the beginning of the process of looking for a partner, I did not revise this description. It is as I wrote it more than a year before this book was published.

Survival—3, Average

From my average need to survive, I still have a hormonal interest in sex: I am interested, but I am not driven. I want a woman who has at least as high a hormonal interest in sex as I have, and if she has more interest, fine. I think it would be enjoyable to be pushed a little sexually, so I do not want someone who has less interest in sex than I have.

I have no financial problems, and I would want a woman who also is financially secure enough not to have to depend on me entirely. I want a woman with whom I can share my money but who is satisfied with a comfortable, but not extravagant, lifestyle. I will continue to work, but I have almost complete control over what I do. I don't mind if a woman works a little or, better yet, can work with me, but I do not want a woman who works so much that we cannot be together to do what we want when we want.

I want a healthy woman who does not worry about health, who is not overly concerned with what she eats, and for whom food or fancy dining is not a major part of her life. I am an involved father and grandfather, but I am not dependent on my children or grandchildren for companionship. I do not want a woman with small children or even dependent children. As an active part of my life, child care is over and I want someone who feels the same way and is in the same situation as I am. Finally, since I fly a lot and live in an earthquake area, I do not want someone so worried about survival that she is uncomfortable with where I live and the way I live.

Love and Belonging—4, Above Average

I don't have a great need for people to satisfy my need to belong. I don't like large social gatherings, and I do not particularly like meeting or making conversation with strangers unless it is part of my work, where I like it very much. I don't get lonely if I have one special person to love who loves me, and I am capable of being by myself with no discomfort if I know that when I reach out someone is there.

What I need most is a woman with whom I can share my quality world with no fear of being criticized or put down. To me, her willingness to share quality worlds is the essence of both friendship and love, and I need that very much in any woman with whom I develop a relationship. Since sexual love is what I want, and sex, for me, is dependent on physical attraction, I want a woman who is attractive and keeps fit.

With someone I love, I am very affectionate and I like this love and affection to be easily and pleasurably reciprocated. One of the painful parts of being single is sleeping alone and I hate it. I like to have a person who is willing to wake up at night to talk and love. I like to be creative and I want a creative lover, one who has no inhibitions, who thinks that anything either person wants to do is fine and does not think sex is something to be bestowed for good behavior or withheld for punishment.

Basically, I want a friend, someone I can enjoy just being with. People say I am a person who they like to do nothing with. I think this is possible to find in a woman. I like to do things on the spur of the moment, and I want someone who goes along, not someone who stops to think of all the reasons not to do it.

Power—4, Above Average

I want people to listen to me and I am willing to listen to them. I don't like people telling me what to do and I do not like telling anyone else what to do. I am moderately competitive, but I do not want to compete in any way with anyone who is close to me. My need for power is well satisfied in my work; I do not need to satisfy it in my personal life. I don't punish, criticize, or put people down, and I do not like anyone to try to do this with me. I do not differentiate between the sexes as far as power goes. I like women and I hire them in my organization, where leadership roles are always open to them.

I don't like the trappings of power like expensive cars, clothes, jewelry, and showing off by spending money. I do, however, want a woman who is well dressed and is interested in looking good and being in style. If she is interested in what I wear or how I look, that is fine with me, but she has to recognize that for me this is not vital.

I am not a social climber and I would not be interested in a woman who is. I have no interest in meeting the "right" people (I don't even know who they are). I stand up for my rights, but I am not pushy and I do not like pushy people. As I look over what I have described, I don't think I'll have any trouble finding a woman who will go along with me where power is concerned.

Freedom—5, Very High

Here I am a bit of a fanatic. I don't like people to tell me that I can't do something I want to do. I listen and even accept other people's opinions, but when I want to do something that does not hurt anyone, I don't like to have anyone tell me not to do it. Because I recognize that this is the way I am, I am not planning to get married again. But I am open to the fact that this may change if I become involved with someone who wants to marry. But I will not marry anyone who, from the beginning, insists on marriage.

Any woman who wants me has to accept the fact that I will not promise to be exclusive with her. But if I love her, it is likely I will be exclusive. My strong need for freedom leads me to be this way. I believe that love can exist with more than one woman, but I am not sure that sexual love can exist with more than one woman. This is one of the things that I am interested in finding out as I try to establish myself in a new sexual love relationship.

However, I know that the more that I put the woman I love into my quality world, the less desire I have to see anyone else. But I can't put her deeply into my quality world if she makes demands on what I consider my freedom. So for a woman to gain my exclusive love (if that is what she wants), she has to give me my freedom. I think I can find a woman who I can love enough so that she will give this to me, and I intend to try.

Freedom is strongly tied to creativity, and being creative is just about my highest priority. I think creativity in a relationship is what keeps it fresh and exciting, and the creative urge, which is within us all, is most available to us only when we feel free. Since we are all control systems, and all control systems want to be in control, we have to be careful not to attempt to control others but to find ways to control our own lives in creative ways.

Fun—5, Very High

If fun is the reward for learning, as I think it is, and if the hallmark of fun is laughter, then I want to continue to spend my life learning and laughing. One of the reasons my marriage was successful was that we continued to learn, work, and laugh together up to the end. I am not willing to give this up, so a woman has to appreciate what I do and want to share it with me. I am not looking for a rubber stamp to verify my success; I am looking for someone who thinks and works in the same area that I do and wants to join me and do what she can to expand and clarify my work.

I am perfectly happy to help her to do what she does, but at this stage of my life I want someone who is vitally interested in what I do. This requirement makes it hard to meet someone fresh, so I have given up trying to start a relationship with someone who is not aware of what I do. This is somewhat limiting, but I am too old, I have traveled down the control theory/reality therapy/quality management road too long, and there is too much history and too little time to start anew.

As far as laughing and joking are concerned, they are vitally important to me. Without a lot of laughter, I lose interest; I can't conceive of a relationship without it. I think I will be able to find a woman who can laugh as we work and share ideas and who also appreciates that creativity is strongly sustained not only by freedom but also by fun.

So there they are, the pictures in my quality world of myself, my potential partner, and our relationship. There is nothing right or wrong about my pictures—it is how I see myself. My quality world is my creation; it is what will determine my life. If some of it is not possible to achieve, I will suffer, and from this suffering I may try to change it.

If you too are looking for a sexual love relationship or trying to improve the one you have, I urge you to write a description of your quality world and be prepared to share it with the person you believe you love. This will give fair warning to your partner of what you are like and, if your partner reciprocates, fair warning of what he or she is like. If your quality worlds are not compatible, don't expect them to change very much. Expect that you and your partner have your work cut out for you, but at least you have a good idea of what you have to do.

I put some work and thought into what I have written here, but it was not hard. In fact, it was enjoyable. I did it not to tell you who I am but to show you a real example of a quality world. I will now share with you the quality world of Carleen Floyd, a woman with whom I have become romantically involved. She agreed to do this because she also believes that we should try to find out if our need-strength profiles and our quality worlds are compatible.

Carleen's Personality Profile and Quality World

Based on what I know about myself, the following is a description of the pictures in my quality world of myself, my prospective mate, and our relationship. Most of these pictures have been in my quality world for many years; some are new pictures; and some are pictures I may have to remove as I continue to grow and evaluate their need satisfaction. But at the moment, what I have written is an accurate description.

I have a 35344 personality or need-strength profile. I am average in survival, high in love and belonging, average in power, and above average in freedom and fun.

Survival—3, Average

Since survival is connected with the drive to reproduce, and sex is part of that process, I believe my sex drive is normal to high. Mostly, I think of myself as a sensual, exciting woman who enjoys lovemaking, especially if it includes exchanging lots of affection. I am fairly uninhibited and creatively expressive in my sexual play and I expect the same from my partner. Although orgasm is very important to me, I consider it only one small part of the total sexual experience. I also prefer my lover to be slightly less driven by sexual urgency than myself. That way I feel safe because I am in more control of my experience.

Money is a necessary part of survival in our society, and I have enough to be relatively comfortable. I rarely worry about money. I do not waste it and it always seems to be available when I need it. It is important to me to have an independent income. In addition to my full-time job, I have a small business and some investments to add to my retirement income for further security. I want a man who is also financially secure, not worried about his income, and willing to spend some of it having fun, preferably with me.

I am extremely healthy and not overly concerned about becoming ill. I am not an exercise fanatic and not particularly worried about my intake of fuel. I am not overweight and I basically eat when I am hungry. I do not smoke, I do not drink alcohol excessively, and I avoid caffeine altogether.

I am neither a worrier nor am I overly concerned about change. I rather like new horizons and unusual experiences. I am spontaneous and able to pick up and go at a moment's notice. I am a risk taker to a degree. I am interested in a man who keeps himself physically fit and looks after his health. As much as possible, I want him to match my personality profile in the survival need, especially to be willing to take risks too. Since none of this is extreme, I should have no difficulty finding a man who is compatible with my need to survive.

Love and Belonging—5, Very High

I come from a very affectionate family with lots of love and encouragement. I still crave being hugged and kissed, so I need a lot of affection from the man in my life. I like him to tell me he loves me often, as well as everything he likes about me. I am convinced that lovemaking is a twenty-four-hour-a-day activity. It is expressed throughout the day by loving touches; warm, caring looks; little kindnesses; intimate conversations; and cuddling. I want a man who is present for me when he is with me. I like that presence to be time we just enjoy being together doing nothing in particular, our special time away from worldly distractions.

I love being with people in almost every setting except at big parties or in very large crowds, unless they are an audience and I am the presenter. I would rather relate to people individually or in couples. In my work I deal with people, not things. When I find myself alone in my office doing paperwork for too long without human contact, I seek it. It is not that I mind being alone or that I fear it—I even enjoy some solitude every day—but I do not consider myself a loner. I really enjoy the company of a good friend or lover.

I have some very special women friends. I call them my "soul sisters" because we are of like minds. My step-daughter, who is twenty-five, is one of them. I can talk with my "soul sisters" for hours and we never tire of each other. I am looking for their counterpart in a man, someone who understands me and loves me just the way I am and who is of like mind. It is important that our philosophy of life is similar.

Because my love and belonging need rated my highest score, I keep a beautiful picture in my quality world of having a long-term, satisfying relationship wherein I feel completely loved and fulfilled. I can return the love freely without inhibition and without fear of my love being rejected when the intensity of it is overwhelming. I will be sure it is right for me because when we are together I am happier than when we are apart. He knows how it feels to be in my skin and I know how it feels to be in his skin—we are that compatible!

What I also want from a man is complete intimacy. Nothing less will do for me. I am not looking to get married again, nor am I opposed to the idea, but whatever our ultimate status, I need a man who is willing to explore all the possibilities of a deeply intimate relationship with the creativity, honesty, and sense of humor it takes to keep love exciting, alive, and growing. He could expect no less a commitment from me.

Power—3, Average

Most of my power comes from how I feel about myself, not how much I need to control others. I have a positive self-image. I consider myself an attractive woman with the typical Mediterranean's dark, prominent eyes and sallow complexion. As far back as I can remember, I have attracted attention because of my somewhat striking appearance. I am fully aware that I dress to be noticed and use makeup with a dramatic flare. Even though I am over fifty, I look and act vibrant and energetic. I am an artist and I enjoy using my talent to create the best look for me. I am successful because I am good at what I do and because I project a competent and beautiful self-image.

I have virtually no desire to control anyone else. Neither do I put anyone down in order to feel better about myself. I rarely compete for anything with anyone—even when playing a competitive game. I play for the fun of it, and if I lose (as I often do), I really win, because I enjoy the activity and the companionship.

I hate it when anyone makes fun of me seriously or in jest and I especially dislike put-down humor of any kind. Being taken for granted, or being ignored by a lover, is even worse. I want a man who is proud of my accomplishments and talents, not threatened by them, and who understands my lack of competitiveness and does not take advantage of it to get more power for himself. I do not want to be in a power struggle over anything with my mate.

Certain things are important to me and are tied to my self-image and power identity, and when I tell him what they are, I want him to respect them. Aesthetic experiences of all kinds are especially important to me. I am also interested in fashion and looking pretty in clothes not as a symbol of power but for the aesthetic enjoyment of it.

My need for intrinsic power is high, but my need for external power is low. Put together, I think I am average in the strength of this need.

Freedom—4, Above Average

I believe we are all free. The only time we feel a lack of freedom is when we allow someone else to control us. My need for freedom right now is rather strong. In my life I have had varying degrees of freedom over the years, proportionate to the amount of control I perceived others to exert over me. Sometimes in the past, in order to get more freedom, I felt I had to go underground and live a secret life. Now I am living aboveground and the freedom I give myself is matched by the freedom I recognize others possess.

In my relationship with a man, I have no desire to restrict his freedom. What a foolish task for me to attempt, because it is impossible to accomplish! I do not demand exclusivity, for example, because demanding something I cannot control is an unrealistic expectation. He is going to do whatever is most need satisfying for himself anyway, no matter what I expect, and more so if I demand. Therefore, I expect nothing but honesty. If he finds someone he prefers over me, so be it. If his preference is made known to me honestly, then he is gone and I am free to look elsewhere.

When I am completely in love with a man, I have no desire to be with another man, but I still feel free, because it is my choice to remain exclusive. I do not demand it of myself and do not want anyone else to demand it of me; it just happens. If I can fulfill all my needs with one man, why would I look for another? Perhaps for the thrill of conquest? But that is not getting me more freedom; that is getting me more power.

I feel exceedingly free because I am open-minded, accepting, and honest about myself. I want the same from my lover. I know that whenever I lock my mind in one position and refuse to budge on any issue, I become the one locked in while everyone else is merrily doing what they want to do no matter how much I suffer. I happily gave up that kind of thinking a long time ago. I am learning to let it go if it is out of my control. No one can restrict the freedom of my mind and choices I make but myself. Strap me in leg shackles and I will still find a way to be free!

Fun—4, Above Average

I need a man with a good sense of humor, who says funny things at the most unexpected times. I enjoy the spontaneous, the unpredictable, like a surprise letter, a winter vacation in the sun, sex in the middle of the night, Greek olives, the carousel ride at Santa Monica Pier, and a special man to share them with. I like to shop for bargains and have the sheer delight of finding the greatest one.

I laugh much more than I complain and I want a man who does the same. Some people have called me an incurable optimist because I tend to have a positive outlook and a joyfulness about me most of the time. I love learning new things, especially if I am good at doing them. I enjoy live theater, movies, art museums, traveling, and any creative project particularly involving art and design. Even my work is fun for me most of the time.

I want a man who is fun to be with even when we are not doing anything special; someone who likes to listen to me and talks with me about anything and everything; someone I can laugh with and be silly with. At this stage in my life, I am ready to retire from my full-time job, continue to work at what I like occasionally, and have a good time being with a man who loves me joyfully and wants the same things in life as I do.

Comparing Both Our Profiles and Our Quality Worlds

Since we have been together for more than a year and are happier than ever with each other, we believe that our compatible profiles (mine 34455; hers 35344) must have something to do with it. Our quality worlds have a possible power and freedom incompatibility. My need for power is higher but, as Carleen explains, she has no desire to change what others do, so there should be no problem. Both our freedom needs are high, but neither of us has any desire to restrict the other so again there should be no problem. Fun is obviously highly compatible and it turns out to be a strong positive force in our relationship.

Although Carleen and I have no concern about revealing ourselves publicly, part of that willingness is due to our good relationship and our eagerness to teach others what we have learned. We do not suggest that you feel in any way obligated to go public about your life. Under most circumstances sexual love should be a private contract to all except the parties involved. To each other it is best to be truthful, as long as the truth is not used to hurt, such as revealing an affair for the sake of trying to make the offended partner feel inferior, to ask forgiveness, or both. It is not fair to ask your partner to share in the pleasure or pain of what you do if that is hurtful to her or him.

If you are in a relationship, satisfied or not, what Carleen and I have just done is an excellent private exercise for you and your partner. If your partner is willing to do this with you, it can be a powerful beginning to a better relationship or marriage. You can initiate this separately, as I did here, but then I shared it with Carleen and she agreed to do her part. If you think that your partner would be hesitant, I suggest you do as I did and then ask your partner if he or she will do the same.

If your partner is unwilling or, for some personal reason, you do not want to ask him or her to share this with you, you can still do it by yourself and work to change what you can to try to make the relationship better.

7

Total Behavior

Although most of us don't think about it, all we do from birth to death is behave. And all of our behavior is always our best attempt to satisfy the pictures of what we most want from life that previously we put into our quality worlds. Since this book is about what we need to do to find satisfying sexual love, almost all the pictures that relate to love, sex, and staying together have to be satisfying both to ourselves and our sexual partners, not just to ourselves alone. Even though all of our lives we have to make an effort to get along with other people and create pictures in our quality worlds to do so, this effort is never as intense and focused as it is with someone we love.

Obviously, being able to create enough of these mutually satisfying pictures to sustain a good relationship, and then to figure out the behaviors needed to satisfy them, is a very difficult task. Few sexual partners can do it successfully for even a few years, much less for a lifetime. It would help if we could learn much more about how we actually behave. To do this, I now explain total behavior, a control theory explanation of all human behavior that is much different from, and much more useful than, what most of us know. When I say all behavior, I am talking about all conscious behavior that has a purpose. I am not talking about the tiny percentage of behaviors that are automatic, such as coughing or sneezing, or unconscious, such as dreaming.

The Cause of Our Behavior

All of our behavior is generated by the difference between what we want at the time, which is a picture or pictures from our quality world, and what we have, which is what we see going on in the real world. For example, most likely you are reading this book because you have a picture in your quality world of a better love relationship than what you actually have. Driven by this difference between what you want and what you have, you hope this book is a source of helpful information that you can use to get you closer to the relationship you want. What you are doing as you read and think about this book is acting on the real world, to try to move what you have in this world closer to what you want.

Although you are now reading this book in the hopes of finding out what to do to make your love relationship better, this is not the only thing you could have done. You could have chosen to get drunk, a common choice for people who want quick relief from the pain of a bad relationship. You could have chosen to try to find someone else and become involved in an affair, or go so far as to leave your partner. You could have chosen to argue, fight, or withdraw—all very common choices. Although you would not be aware that this is a choice, you could have chosen a physical pain, such as chronic headaches. The list is endless. I mention only these few choices to show that, given the same unsatisfying situation, there are many behaviors, mostly painful, we can choose to try to make things better.

Control theory, therefore, teaches something that most of you are aware of to some extent: When you are faced with an unsatisfying situation in your life, you must behave to try to make it better. You cannot ignore it; you must do something. In some cases you may not be aware of what you are choosing to do. In many cases you are not even aware that what you are doing is a choice. But as I will explain, it is always a choice.

For example, many women who came to me in my practice said that they were depressed. Even though a bad love relationship, usually marriage, is the most common cause of depression in women, when I inquired about their marriage, often they told me it was fine. As we continued to talk about their marriage, because I refused to accept that it was fine, it came out that it was not nearly as good as they wanted it to be. In control theory terms, it was much less satisfying than the marriage picture in their quality world.

Later, as I explained control theory and total behavior to them, they also found out that they were choosing to depress (control theory terminology for depression, which I soon explain). As they became acquainted with total behavior, they found out that if they were choosing to depress, they could make a better choice. Given this option, they then chose to stop depressing. It was my job as a counselor to teach them to make this better choice, and most of the time I was successful in doing this.

All Behavior Is Total and All Behavior Is Chosen

My dictionary defines *behavior* first as "activity" and second as "a response to a stimulus." The first definition is inadequate; the second is wrong. If all we do is behave, it is obvious that behavior is much more than activity. Together with activity, or as I prefer to call it, acting, we always think as we behave, we always feel, and there is always some physiology going on—the four components that make up what is most accurately called total behavior. It is not a response to a stimulus; it is our best attempt to satisfy pictures that we have placed in our quality worlds.

In the first chapter when I discussed the needs, I emphasized our feelings in an effort to show that when we satisfy one or more of the basic needs, the behaviors that we use to satisfy them always feel good. Now you can see that I was talking about the feeling component of any need-satisfying behavior. For example, if you hug and kiss someone you love, the hugging and kissing is the activity. While you are doing it, you are thinking about how much you enjoy doing this and your thoughts may progress to a more intensely satisfying activity. All the while, you feel very good and may even feel better as the behavior intensifies. As all this is going on, your heart and breathing rates may increase and you may involuntarily moan with pleasure, which is the typical physiology associated with this total behavior.

As you think about hugging and kissing and about my claim that we choose all of our total behaviors, you may say that you are not choosing to moan, to increase the rate of your heart or breathing, or even to feel the way you feel. These are just happening as you hug and kiss. What you claim is true. All you are actually choosing is to hug and kiss, the acting, and, as you muse, also thinking about how pleasurable this is. But could you experience the increased heart rate and the intense pleasure if you did not choose to hug, kiss, and think sexy thoughts about someone you care for at the time? No. We can rarely control or choose our feelings or our physiology, but we always can control or choose our conscious actions and thoughts.

This is why we are always in some sort of control of our lives. Where marriage is concerned, this control is effective if we have a happy marriage and ineffective if we have a bad marriage. Therefore, to have a good marriage, we have to be able to make good choices, to think and act much better than we do in a bad marriage. When I counseled the depressed women with the bad marriages, I helped them to make much better acting and thinking choices than they were used to making. I did not attempt to help them to feel better or to have a better physiology (perhaps they were having severe headaches), because control theory teaches that without changing our actions and thoughts, this is impossible.

All we can change and, therefore, must change if we are unsatisfied with our behavior is how we are choosing to act and think. But since making a change in any total behavior necessarily changes that total behavior, it is correct to say that we choose our total behaviors. If we make better acting and thinking choices, we will feel better and have a more healthy physiology and, of course, a better marriage.

Even though it seems awkward at first, from now on I use verbs to describe total behaviors because grammatically all behaviors are designated by verbs, never by nouns or adjectives. Therefore, we choose to depress (an infinitive) or we choose depressing (a gerund). We do not suffer from depression (a noun), and we are never depressed (an adjective). At first glance, this technical grammar may not seem very important, but if you incorporate it into your life, you will soon discover that it is. When you have a bad marriage and you think of yourself as "depressed," or suffering from "depression," you tend to feel helpless, as if this is happening to you from somewhere outside, and you may look around for someone to relieve your pain or for an addicting drug like alcohol to take away your pain.

If instead you say, "I am choosing to depress," you are almost forced to think of making an effort to make a better and more active choice than to sit around moping and hoping that someone or something will come along to help. You may begin to choose to think, "Maybe I ought to do something to help myself," and then actually add some effective action to this thought. It is this effective voluntary effort that this chapter is all about.

What Is Misery and Why Do We Choose It?

Misery is the feeling component of a group of common total behaviors that most of us choose when our lives are not in effective control, such as when we are unsatisfied in a relationship. The most common misery we choose is depressing, but we can also choose to withdraw, complain, go crazy, drink, or use drugs. We may choose to become anxious, tense, fearful, compulsive, and/or sick, a gamut of behaviors commonly chosen when we believe our marriage is not living up to its quality world picture. Usually preceding these behaviors, and sometimes accompanying them, is *angering*, the basic and most common of all the total behaviors we choose when things are not the way we want them to be.

As difficult as it is for most of us to accept, we choose miserable, total behaviors because we believe they are the best choices we can make at the time. The particular misery you choose is probably based on what you have discovered works best for you or what you have seen other miserable people choosing. For example, I once counseled an eight-year-old girl who told me that when she grew up she was going to have migraine headaches like her mother.

But finding out why you choose this or that misery is not particularly important. Control theory teaches that what is important is to figure out how to choose a more effective behavior, because until you do, you will continue to choose to suffer. Instead of expending time and energy trying to discover why you chose your particular misery, expend it on choosing a more effective total behavior.

Everyone who chooses to depress in a bad relationship wants to be treated better. Suppose you are a woman who is unable to get the love or attention you want from your husband. As much as you may want to, you cannot ignore what is going on. The first behavior that comes to your mind is to anger, but if you choose to anger, in most cases you will discover that angering makes things worse. It leads to fights, often to violence, and you, as the weaker party, are usually the loser.

But you cannot just stop angering. If you want to stop angering, you have to choose another behavior that will, in effect, restrain it by replacing it. You have another behavior immediately available, which you learned when you were small: You choose to depress.

You know how you act, think, and feel when you choose to depress. Although you are usually not aware of it, your physiology is slowed down and you do not feel physically fit. Depressing is so familiar, so much a part of our common experience, that there is no synonym for it in the dictionary. You have been choosing it since childhood when you are frustrated, and you have done so for three reasons: (1) to restrain the angering that you know will make things worse; (2) as a cry for help from your husband or anyone else who might help; and (3) as a way to avoid doing something better, but something that will take a lot of work, such as leaving your husband.

The first reason, restraining the angering, I have already explained. The second is obvious; almost all of us are screaming for help when we choose to depress. Few of us choose suffering and then try to hide it. The third reason is less obvious and needs to be explained. For example, friends with whom you share your misery tell you, "Leave him," and you agree. But in the same breath you say, "I would but I'm too depressed to do it." Although control theory teaches that depressing is a choice, it is neither an easy choice nor is it easy to make a better choice.

If you want to stop the misery you are choosing, you have to summon up the strength to make a better choice, and it is the relationship with a good helping person such as a counselor who knows control theory that can give you the strength to make this better choice. To encourage you to stop depressing and do something better, the counselor will also make it clear to you that depressing takes a lot of energy and gets you nowhere.

But in my experience, most people have more strength than they realize, especially when they learn enough control theory to know what's going on. They can use this strength to help themselves or use the encouragement of good friends and supportive family to try to choose a better behavior. What the knowledge of control theory can offer is hope. It is the hopelessness of the thinking component of total behaviors like depressing that robs you of your strength and makes life seem so difficult and bleak.

You are probably thinking that this is impossible. You are not choosing to feel this way; it is happening to you. And you might add that no one in her right mind would choose to feel this way. What you do not realize is that you are no longer in your "right mind." You feel enervated, as if your mind has lost its ability to direct you to help yourself as you used to do.

Now that you know about total behavior, you know that you don't have to continue to choose to depress. You know that a better choice is available any time you want to make it. In almost all instances, there are a wide variety of much more effective and, eventually, more satisfying, marriage-improving or marriage-dissolving behaviors than the painful and ineffective choice to depress.

Suggestions for Action

Take the time to say to yourself and keep saying to yourself, "My marriage is unsatisfying and, for a long time, I have been choosing to depress (perhaps along with some other ineffective, miserable behaviors such as anxieting, angering, criticizing, complaining, withdrawing, and drinking), but now that I realize that I am choosing what I am doing, I am going to try to make a better choice."

It may take a while to come up with a better choice. But if you keep reminding yourself that you are choosing the painful total behavior you are feeling, you will begin to think harder about figuring out a more effective behavior. As you do, these thoughts will give you hope, and the self-chosen hopelessness that has dominated your marriage will lose its power.

As you gain a little hope, you will begin to realize that what I have said is true: All the pain that you have been choosing has served no good, long-term purpose. You have kept your life together by restraining your anger. You have made your cry for help and you have been able to excuse yourself for your lack of doing something better. But time continues to pass and you are really no better off where your marriage is concerned. So why continue? Now that you have learned a little control theory, why not try it? Let me now suggest a specific scenario that you may try. There is no guarantee that it will work, but it certainly will not make your marriage any worse than it is now.

Let's assume that the vast majority of women who have locked themselves into unsatisfying marriages are not married to ogres. You do not live in fear of your life and there are small islands of satisfaction in a sea of discontent. This point is important: What makes it bad is not so much the daily pain; it is that you have lost hope that it will ever be much better. But do you have to think this way? No. These thoughts are voluntary, and you can change them right now if you wish to try.

To begin, wait for a time when you are alone with your partner and your relationship is in neutral, that is, you are not arguing or fighting. Then, using a gentle, inquiring tone of voice, ask your partner the following question: "Right now are you satisfied with our marriage? Please just answer yes or no." If he says, "No" or

"It's okay," as I assume he will, say either, "I agree" or "Okay is not enough for me." In the unlikely case that he says, "Yes," say, "Well, you may be satisfied, but I'm not."

If he asks what's wrong with the marriage or why are you so unhappy, or makes any reference to what in the marriage is not working, say, "I don't want to talk about what's wrong because it doesn't make any difference whether we agree or disagree. Talking about what's wrong is not going to change anything. It's like talking about a flat tire; you can talk forever, but it stays flat."

As he waits for what you are going to say next, say, "What I plan to do is to try to get something going in this marriage as soon as possible that's better than what we have. If you want to work with me, fine. If you don't, I am going to stop moping and stop complaining about you, me, or anybody or anything and try to get something going that we both enjoy. Life is too short to be unhappy, and I have been unhappy long enough."

At this point, if there is anything left of the marriage, he will wake up and begin to pay attention. He may ask, perhaps with some alarm, as he too is used to the usual, stable misery that has become your marriage, what you are going to do. If he does, be prepared to ask with a smile that conveys the possibility that he too wants something better, "What would you like me to do? I'll do anything you say and I am prepared to do it right now."

In the unlikely case that he suggests sex, be careful. For many men sex is the marriage cure-all. Your sex life is not insufficient because you don't desire sex or are incapable of enjoying it. It is bad because you are not friends; most of the time one or both of you is inconsiderate of the other and you do almost nothing together that you both enjoy. This is the goal of what I am suggesting. If it is successful, sex will improve.

After you pose the I'll do anything question, if he says nothing, or says he doesn't know what to suggest, be prepared to continue with no help from him. Don't be surprised if you draw a blank. If he were more aware and/or more creative, your marriage would be in better shape. Expect this to happen and tell him that you are not depending on him.

Then give him a hug and a kiss and tell him, "Don't worry. I'll figure something out. But I'm sure that somewhere in your brain are some pictures of what we could do together that we would both enjoy. Look, if you feel like it, we can talk again tomorrow. This is enough for now. Keep in mind what I said. I'm tired of being unhappy and complaining all the time. I want to be happy and I plan to do something to find some happiness. I hope you'll help me figure out something we can do together, but if you won't, I'm still going ahead."

This is a big start, so don't push too far. You know enough about your needs to have a good idea of what he needs too. You have worked out your need-strength profile and taken an educated guess at his. You have found that while you and he are not supercompatible, there is some compatibility. You have figured out what is in your quality world where marriage is concerned, and you have a good idea of what is in his. If he wants to talk further, which he may if you stop depressing, complaining, and criticizing, then your best chance is to ask him to read this book. If he will, you may be on your way to a more satisfying marriage.

At this point you've done about all you can. If he is still not interested in working with you to improve your relationship, go ahead without him.

8

How We Relate to Each Other

In the last chapter, I talked about hope. Here I would like to add that hope is more than the belief that things may not get worse. Hope is believing that things will get better. We'll do things we both enjoy and do them often enough so they become a part of our lives we can count on. Not all the time, not even a lot, but at a minimum almost every day there is a bright spot, some real closeness, a time when we're more than accepting of each other—we are actually enjoying each other's company. It's a time of no tension, neither partner complaining or making demands, a time to relax and just enjoy being with each other. To some this may sound idyllic, but why not try for it? If you don't, there is no hope.

When tension arises in relationships other than marriage, you can just walk away for a while, and you're both relieved. When the tension lifts, you get back together. Since you are not tied to each other, you have no pressing reason to keep trying to change the other. But in marriage, walking away is harder than in any other relationship, so hard that it is not usually an option. Each wants to have the last word, to argue to the bitter end, to keep trying to change the other, to get the other to admit wrong, to blame the other for not loving, not being sensitive to "my needs," not trying to work things out, for trying "to get away from me."

What is needed is not so much a way to deal with problems as they arise but a greater understanding of the ways we relate to each other so that fewer problems occur in the relationship. Once an argument erupts, there are few good ways to deal with it.

The Four Ways We Relate to Each Other

As we became civilized, four basic human relationships emerged: (1) love and friendship, (2) counseling, (3) teaching, and (4) managing. For a successful marriage, love and friendship is critical; counseling and teaching (as I soon explain) are helpful; but if either the husband, wife, or both attempt to manage the other, the consequences are almost always disastrous for the marriage.

Love and Friendship

The foundation for a happy marriage is sexual love based on close friendship. Good sex is built on anything each can do to give the other physical pleasure. The partners must talk freely to each other and agree on what is acceptable in bed. Close friendship is built on a lot of comfortable hugging, kissing, and caressing, talking to each other easily and enjoyably, sharing common interests, and, especially, doing things together where there is some learning and improvement. The more compatible their need-strength profiles and their quality worlds, the more this happens.

Couples who don't talk or share can live together and still be reasonably satisfied if they have good friends with whom they can talk comfortably and even intimately. This, however, is only satisfying; it does not provide the happiness with each other that both need for a good marriage. There is little more that can be said about love and friendship except that a happy marriage needs a lot of both. If you have to learn from scratch how to love and be friends with your partner, there is little chance for a good relationship.

Counseling

Counseling is accurately defined as one person helping another with some sort of a life problem, provided the person being helped wants and asks for it. It is not counseling for one to tell the other that he or she needs help: "Here's what you have to do." This is managing, usually disastrous for the marriage. If one tells the other that he or she needs help and advises the other to get help from a friend, relative, or professional, this can be positive as long as the partner who gives that advice is pretty sure the other partner wants help. If you have any idea that he or she doesn't want help, do not offer it; it will be seen as another way to manage. And you certainly cannot force help on a partner who does not want it. This can lead to violence and is often the precipitating cause of spousal abuse.

The counseling method that I have found most useful is described in detail in my book *Reality Therapy*. It is usually taught to professional counselors, but it lends itself well to partners who want to help each other because it is actually a way to apply control theory to a personal problem.

Assuming that there is some warmth and support in the marriage, the counseling partner should ask the partner seeking help what he or she wants in the marriage. Take your time and ask him or her to explain as clearly as possible what seems to be missing. No matter what he or she says (and this is why it is hard to counsel a partner), the counseling partner should not get defensive, just listen.

Then ask, "Is what you are choosing to do getting you what you just said you want?" If it is not, as is usually the case, ask, "If you are not getting what you want with what you are choosing to do, can we, together, work out a new way that is acceptable to both of us? I'll help you in any way I can. Let's see if we can come up with something that will work." Being a partner is an advantage as you take this step. You are able to address the problem directly, not indirectly, as would be the case with an outside professional counselor or even a friend. There are both advantages and disadvantages to counseling a partner, and in practice they may even out.

If you follow exactly what I suggest—no criticism, no blame, no rehashing or digging up the past, dealing with the problem as it exists now, and looking for better things to do together—you can help each other. This is the help that lasts because you gain confidence in your ability to help each other and the hope that goes along with this confidence. You learn in practice that you don't have to choose to be miserable; you can solve problems. But I repeat: Attempt this only if the partner or partners agree to your help.

Teaching

Teaching is easier than counseling, and spouses frequently teach partners. If the pupil-spouse wants to learn from the teacher-spouse, this is a strong source of joy in a marriage. My wife told me that I needed to learn a lot about writing. But in the beginning I didn't agree and angered because it was laborious to make all the corrections she suggested. Therefore, her initial attempts to teach me did not work. This changed dramatically when I learned to use a word processor. Then I became eager for her instruction because the changes were not only easy but fun. This is an example of how teaching can go wrong and then go right through no fault of the spouse-teacher.

Teaching in a relationship as sensitive as a marriage must take place in an atmosphere in which the teacher does not criticize the pupil for being slow to catch on or for anything else the student does that is not what the teacher wants. Even if the student asks for criticism, it is better not to offer it. The student is likely to perceive the teacher-spouse as attempting to run a power trip on the learner, and any attempt to gain power in a marriage is harmful. The power balance of any marriage is very delicate. Both partners must work hard to find and maintain the correct balance of power for that marriage. So teaching is like counseling in that the pupil-spouse needs to want to learn.

On the other hand, if either partner wants to learn something from another source, he or she should go ahead and enroll in a class or seek a teacher. This does not unbalance the marriage and in fact is usually very good. If the partners care about each other and, to some extent, share what each is learning, this always helps the marriage.

If, however, one partner learns a great deal and the other stands pat and has no interest, this bad situation takes a lot out of what was already a joyless relationship. What is best is a lot of shared learning, which is a wonderful way to bring and keep joy in any relationship.

Managing

Of all the tasks we attempt in life, successfully managing another person or other people is the most difficult. In marriage, it should not be attempted at all—it is a marriage killer. Even done well, and done with a partner who does not seem to mind or even seems interested, it is a threat to marriage because the managed partner resents being thrust into an unequal power situation in which he or she is the victim. Attempts at managing on the part of one or both partners is by far the main reason marriages fail.

When we think of managing, mostly we think of work, where we are all managed, but it is also the essence of what teachers do in schools, what parents do as they raise children, and, unfortunately, what too many husbands and wives try to do to each other. Done properly, as when the manager convinces the managed that his agenda is good for them, it can work well in business, at school, or with raising children. But in marriage, no matter how well it is done, it fails miserably.

Basically, there is only one kind of management in the world: boss-management. The essence of boss-management is that the boss tells the person he or she is attempting to manage what to do and how to do it. The boss evaluates the progress and then uses rewards and punishments to coerce the other to do what is wanted. Bosses tend to use punishments far more than rewards (rewards are not good either, but they are better than punishments) and the relationship between the boss and the bossed quickly becomes adversarial and usually gets more adversarial as time passes.

In marriage, the punishments the boss-spouse uses are mostly angry criticism and/or withdrawal or threats of withdrawal. The punished spouse retaliates in kind, and more and more they become adversaries, if not enemies.

As adversaries, they may not talk, refuse sex, criticize, complain, drink, and abuse—all the well-known things couples do to each other in an unhappy marriage where bossing or attempted bossing is the norm. Bossing is the main way that people attempt to satisfy their need for power, and people with high power needs that they are unable to satisfy outside of marriage rarely succeed at marriage. They boss too much.

If you are in a relationship but still unmarried, after you are satisfied that you and your mate are reasonably genetically compatible, look for bossing. If it exists this early, it is usually fatal to the marriage because experience teaches that it gets worse as time goes on. The marriage may not end, but bossing will erase any chance for happiness. The problem is that when people with average or low power needs are bossed in a loving or caring way in the early months of marriage, they may not be uncomfortable. The bossing may be misinterpreted as caring.

But no matter how loving it is, it is not caring; it is control. And as control systems, none of us wants to be controlled by others. Eventually we will all fight for control, and that fight destroys the relationship. Some of us fight directly, others indirectly with illness, pains and aches, and most often depressing. But whatever the controlled partner chooses, the marriage suffers serious damage.

Most of you reading this book are probably married, and the unhappiness in your marriage is mostly caused by bossing and the resultant fight for control. This is easy to see but very hard to do something about. To escape from bossing, the first thing to do is to stop the struggle.

Tell the boss partner that you are not going to fight, but you also are not going to do as you are told unless the boss-spouse can explain clearly why what is asked is good for you.

For example, suppose you, as the wife, need more help with the children but your husband insists that the children are your job. If you protest, he will punish you in some way, usually by withdrawing love. The picture in your quality world is of sharing some of the child care; in his, you are the main caregiver. The result of the struggle (and this is only one of a myriad of such struggles in bossed marriages) is that you and he are both reducing the size of the other's picture in your quality worlds, and as this reduction takes place the marriage sours.

If you can gather the strength, you might try telling your partner, "Talk to me, explain to me, help me, listen to me, but don't tell me what to do. If you continue, I am not going to fight; it does no good and we both lose. But believe me, I won't do what you say unless I agree or unless we talk it over and I see your point." (Don't do this if your partner is violent. If you can't settle for what you have, consider divorce. No marriage is worth a beating.)

As you read this you may say to yourself, I have been telling him this for years but he doesn't listen; it's like talking to the wall. Yes, you may have been telling him this, but usually you were still fighting in some way or other and the active power struggle continued unabated. Now you need to do this without fighting. It's very hard, but it is the only way that this advice will work.

What you are trying to do has more of a chance for success if it is not seen as a subtle counterattack, so do not initially refer to any of the obvious marriage problems. Say, "We know how to argue, fight, and hurt each other. Let's try to enjoy being with each other for a change." Then try to figure out something that you have not done before; be creative and a little unpredictable. Creativity in marriage is so vital that it is to this marriage-saving behavior that I now turn.

The Control Theory Explanation of Creativity

We are continually and amazingly creative. But as we look at all the obvious and marvellous creativity, it is hard for most of us to place ourselves in the category of creators. And when we are in a difficult situation such as an unhappy marriage, we certainly don't feel creative. We stick to a set of habitual behaviors like fighting, withdrawing, or depressing that seem so natural yet so ineffective and uncreative. But it is at these difficult times that we must become more creative, to try to instill something new into the marriage that will bring us together. Otherwise, the marriage, divorce or not, will fail.

Control theory teaches that we are all creative all the time. If you watch yourself carefully as you go through a day, you will see frequent evidence of this capacity. Think of what you say—Doesn't its creativity surprise you once in a while? Think of the tone of your voice—Didn't you create it effortlessly to help you make a point? Picture the expression on your face that conveys your feelings—Isn't this sometimes a new and creative expression? Where does all this creativity come from? You don't consciously plan it. It just seems to happen.

Inside our brain, we all have a creative system that is constantly reorganizing our behavioral capacity in an attempt to arrive at something new or different. We see this system in operation most clearly in our dreams. We don't choose our dreams; they happen. Yet, often in some very unusual way, most of them relate to our lives, often to some problem with which we are struggling. But a problem is just another way of saying that there is, as in a bad marriage, a big difference between the picture of what we want and what we perceive we have. And as I have explained, we must try to act to reduce this difference whenever it occurs.

But what if you do not know what to do to reduce this difference? You have two main choices: You can choose some familiar painful, ineffective behavior such as to depress, or you can try to figure out a new behavior that you have never tried before. If you make up your mind to try something new, don't expect it to pop right into your mind. In fact, don't even strain to figure something out. Creativity is not achieved by mental effort.

Once you make up your mind to try to find something new, just let your mind rest (which is actually doing something). Remind yourself that if you just let the problem simmer without depressing, fighting, or whining, you may get an idea. Go about your business for a while as positively as you can. This may not seem like much, but it is considerably more than doing nothing.

Then be open to anything, no matter if at first blush it seems totally different from what you have tried before, especially if it seems it would be fun. For example, I just let my brain tinker gently with what I might advise a wife to do with a husband who won't pull his weight with the kids, and the following came to mind. With the help of the kids, create a little musical play in which the kids ask Dad, with a song, to please help take care of them. Have one of the kids play you and lay it on thick as he or she sings, "I am going to run away if you don't help," and show the kid playing you packing a suitcase. In your play, suggest something specific that Dad can do with little effort. If you don't ask for too much, you may get more than you expect.

Doing something like this will break the tension and may lead to an increase in loving attention later that night as Dad tries to show his appreciation for what you have created. What I am trying to show with this example is not that I am particularly creative or that you need to be particularly creative. It is just that if you give your brain a chance, as I did mine, the creative system functions. Be prepared for any number of stupid or worthless thoughts, but don't criticize yourself no matter what comes to mind. Self-criticism turns the creative system off. Be patient and give yourself time. Your creative system will produce.

Conflict

Of all the situations you encounter in your life, conflict is the most distressing. Conflict occurs when you have two contradictory pictures in your quality world and there is no way to reconcile them. For example, you want to leave the marriage because you are not getting enough love and attention but you do not want to break up the family. Your husband is a good provider and a good father. In this situation, there is no behavior that will work—you can't both leave and stay—and usually no one can help you. When you are in a conflict, no matter how much you choose to suffer, the conflict remains. Except for restraining the angering, the suffering is in vain.

Again, the best place to look for help is your own creative system. It may offer you a new behavior in the form of a new idea. For example, it may tell you to leave and see what happens, an idea so drastic and seemingly impulsive that it seems creative to you. Remember, your creative system does not have to come up with something new to the universe, just something new to *you* at this time. As a good friend of mine says, "When you invent the wheel, it's still an exciting invention. It doesn't matter that you weren't first."

I know when we are depressing or withdrawing, action is the last thing we think about. And as long as we believe that our misery is happening to us, we are stuck. Control theory is a way to get unstuck—there is always something to do. Listen to your creative system; don't excuse yourself by saying it's not your fault. It doesn't matter whose fault it is. What matters is that someone has to step in and make a change, and you, as the one most dissatisfied, are the logical person to do it. If you don't, no one else will.

When I was beginning this book, I asked in my *Institute for Control Theory, Reality Therapy and Quality Management Newsletter,* which is mailed to about 1,000 people, for readers to send in anything they do that has made their marriage happy. I expected to get a lot of answers, but the responses were few and very sparse. I have wondered about this a great deal. Are there so few happy marriages? This may be the case, but I think the answer is something else. I think that what makes a marriage happy is, for most satisfied couples, so ordinary that few thought they had significant ideas.

Those who wrote stressed that they are good friends and make an effort to remain good friends. They don't let misunderstandings take root and become problems; they talk and listen to each other even when they are upset. Some, but not all, mentioned sex. Those who did said they continued to be willing learners and listeners and tried to be creative in bed, but it was the friendship that kept the sex good. These couples confirm a major message of this book.

One of the few extensive responses came from a couple who have been happily married for more than twenty-six years. The response was so appropriate and well written that I would like to close this book by sharing it:

1. We have had at least five different relationships with each other over the twenty-six years.
2. Celebrate the presence of each other many times each day: excited greetings, enthusiasm on the phone, frequent "I love you's," singing songs about each other . . .
3. Always create dates with each other even during the child-rearing years and the busiest of times.
4. Nurture each other. Look for ways to support each other physically and emotionally; for

example, make favorite meals, drive each other to work during storms, consult about business, give massages when watching TV.

5. Take the risk of telling each other what you want and also risk telling each other what you see as not right.

6. Love each other unconditionally. Don't hold out expectations that either raise or lower the amount of love. Love must be freely given.

7. Give freedom to be his or her own person. Accept differences. Honor the boundaries between who one is and who the other is.

8. Look to each other as best friends. Day after day, think and act together as best buddies.

9. Know how to laugh, be silly, and have fun together, with no concern about being embarrassed; for example, speaking in made-up foreign languages, humming and squeezing each other to make songs.

10. Keep sex lively and always growing in mutually agreed-on experimentation.

11. Enjoy making lists together.

I am impressed with how much thought and effort this couple has put into their happy marriage. This does not mean that it has all been rosy; there are no totally rosy marriages. But this couple, without reading this book, confirms most of what I have written. What interests me most about their list is the first point, their claim to have had at least five different relationships in the last twenty-six years. I wondered what these were and asked for more detail.

Here is their description of the various roles that each has played in the marriage:

1. She is a young, bright, serious, protected, inexperienced college student.

   He is a young, creative, rebellious, lively, high school teacher.

2. She is an earth mother, bearing a child, a wonderful cook, weaver, and craftswoman.

   He is an alternative-culture community activist, creating new forms and systems in schools and neighborhoods.

3. She is an entry-level career woman, provider of family income, leader in her organization and community.

   He is out of institutionalized work life, gives primary care to their child, a poet, thinker, into meditation.

4. She is an experienced executive, a national leader in her profession, with a fairly high income, a role model to their teenage daughter.

   He is an entrepreneur, coowner of a construction company, active in church leadership, staff development in social service agency.

5. She is an executive, developing body awareness, foreign language, and new spiritual dimensions, with a deep appreciation for her husband.

   He is a business consultant, pioneering new methodologies for organizations to operate effectively, with a deep appreciation for his wife.

Both were aware of the need for new life roles in any long and necessarily changing relationship and were willing to make the effort to create these roles. What they have done is so much more satisfying than doing the same things with a variety of mates through affairs and multiple marriages.

Will You Help?

If you have been helped by this book, I would like to find out what it was that helped you. The only way that I can get this information is if you write and tell me. I may not be able to answer your individual letters if I get a lot of them, but I will put together a composite answer that I am sure will be both interesting and useful and mail it to all who write.

Write me at:

William Glasser, Inc.
P.O. Box 3230
Canoga Park, California 91396-3230